1·800·ZIGGY®

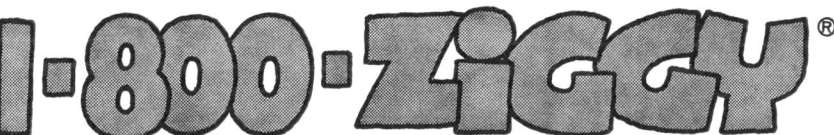

OTHER ZIGGY BOOKS

Ziggy & Friends
Ziggy Faces Life
Ziggy's Big Little Book
Life Is Just a Bunch of Ziggys
Alphabet Soup Isn't Supposed to Make Sense
Ziggy's Place
Ziggy's Ups and Downs
Ziggy in the Fast Lane
Ziggy's Follies
Ziggy's School of Hard Knocks
Ziggy on the Outside Looking In ...
Look Out World ... Here I Come!
Ziggy ... A Rumor in His Own Time
A Day in the Life of Ziggy ...
The Ziggy Treasury
Encore! Encore!!
Ziggy's Star Performances

1-800-ZIGGY®

MY NUMBER IS IN THE BOOK... BUT I THINK I HAVE AN UNLISTED LIFE!

by Tom Wilson

Andrews and McMeel
A Universal Press Syndicate Company
Kansas City

ZIGGY® is a trademark of Ziggy & Friends, Inc. Distributed internationally by Universal Press Syndicate.

1-800-ZIGGY copyright © 1994 by Ziggy & Friends, Inc. All rights reserved. Printed in the United States of America. No part of this book may be used or reproduced in any manner whatsoever without written permission except in the case of reprints in the context of reviews. For information write Andrews and McMeel, a Universal Press Syndicate Company, 4900 Main Street, Kansas City, Missouri 64112.

ISBN: 0-8362-1749-7

Library of Congress Catalog Card Number: 93-80904

ATTENTION: SCHOOLS AND BUSINESSES

Andrews and McMeel books are available at quantity discounts with bulk purchase for educational, business, or sales promotional use. For information, write to: Special Sales Department, Andrews and McMeel, 4900 Main Street, Kansas City, Missouri 64112.

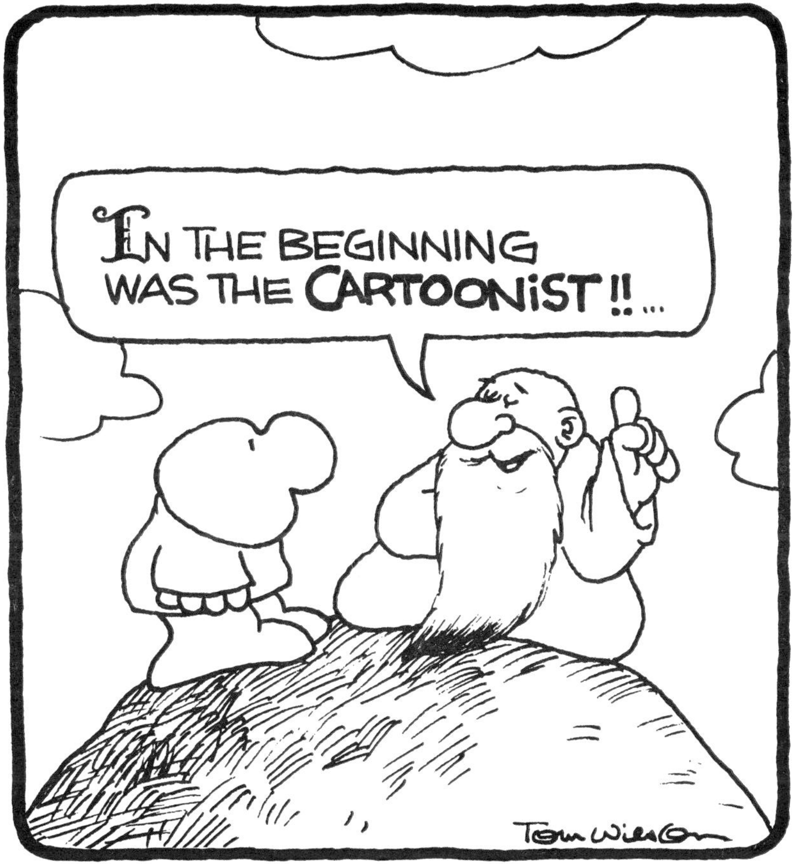
IN THE BEGINNING WAS THE CARTOONIST!!...
TOM WILSON

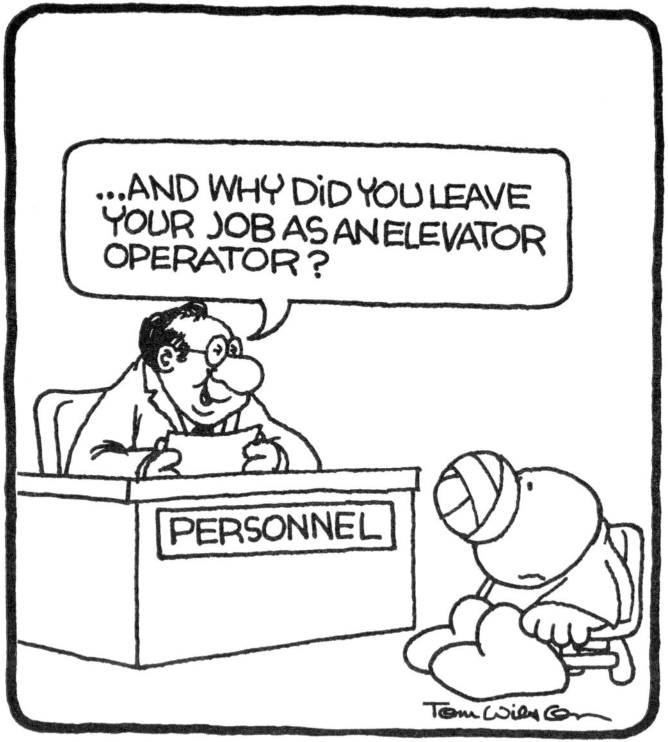
...AND WHY DID YOU LEAVE YOUR JOB AS AN ELEVATOR OPERATOR?
PERSONNEL
Tom Wilson

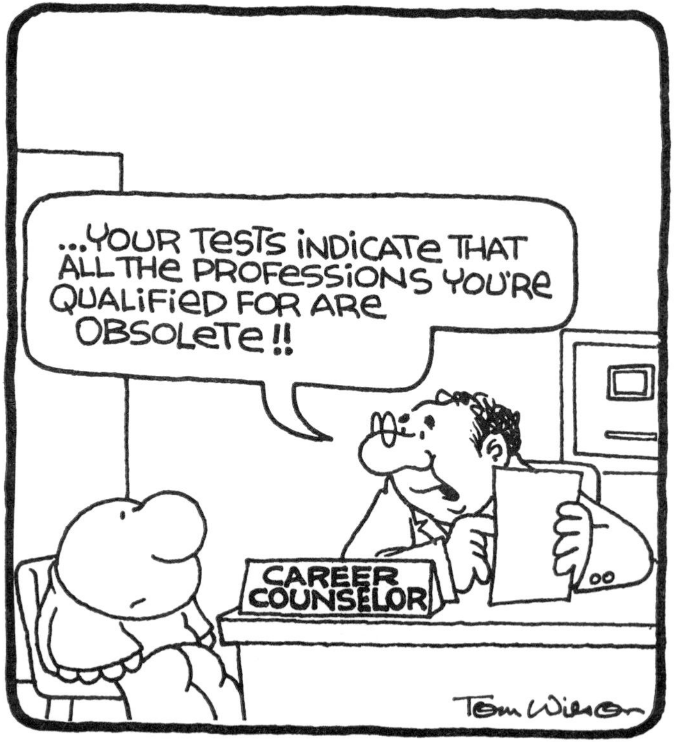
...YOUR TESTS INDICATE THAT ALL THE PROFESSIONS YOU'RE QUALIFIED FOR ARE OBSOLETE!!
CAREER COUNSELOR
Tom Wilson

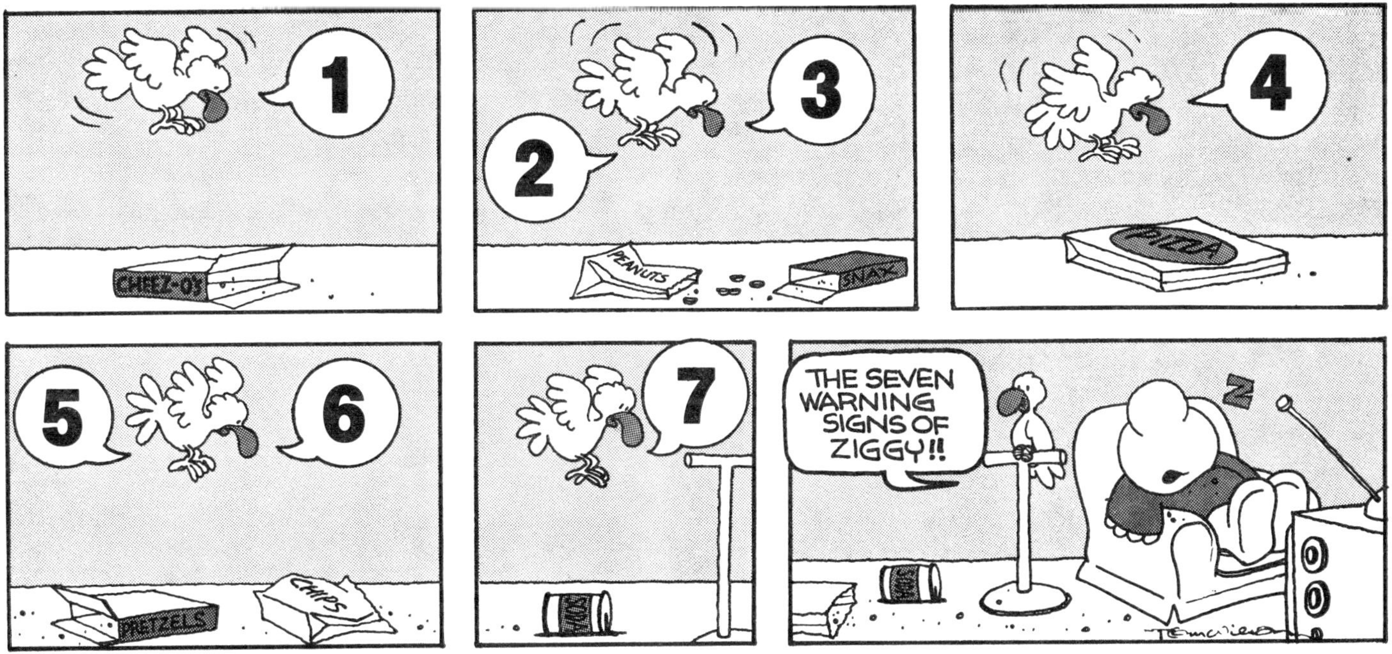
1
2
3
4
5
6
7
THE SEVEN WARNING SIGNS OF ZIGGY!!
CHEEZ-OS
PEANUTS
SNAX
PIZZA
PRETZELS
CHIPS

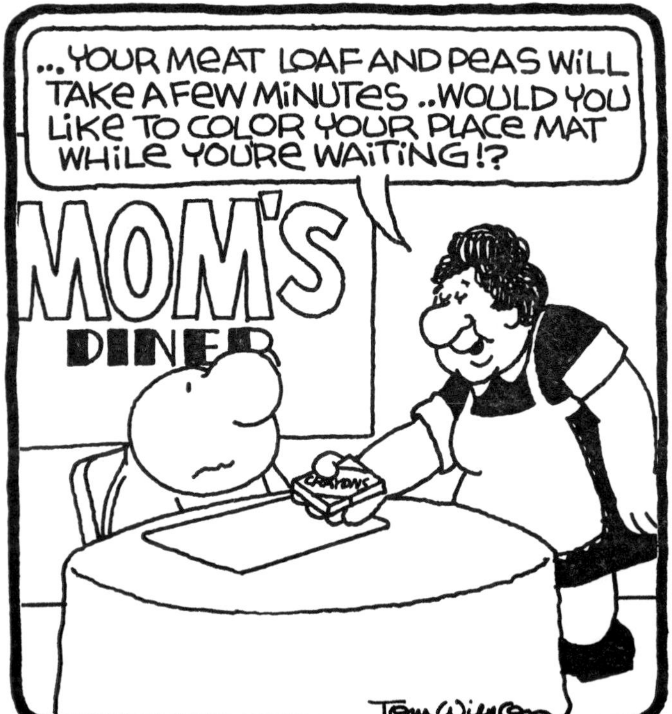
...YOUR MEAT LOAF AND PEAS WILL TAKE A FEW MINUTES ..WOULD YOU LIKE TO COLOR YOUR PLACE MAT WHILE YOU'RE WAITING!?
MOM'S
DINER
CRAYONS
Tom Wilson

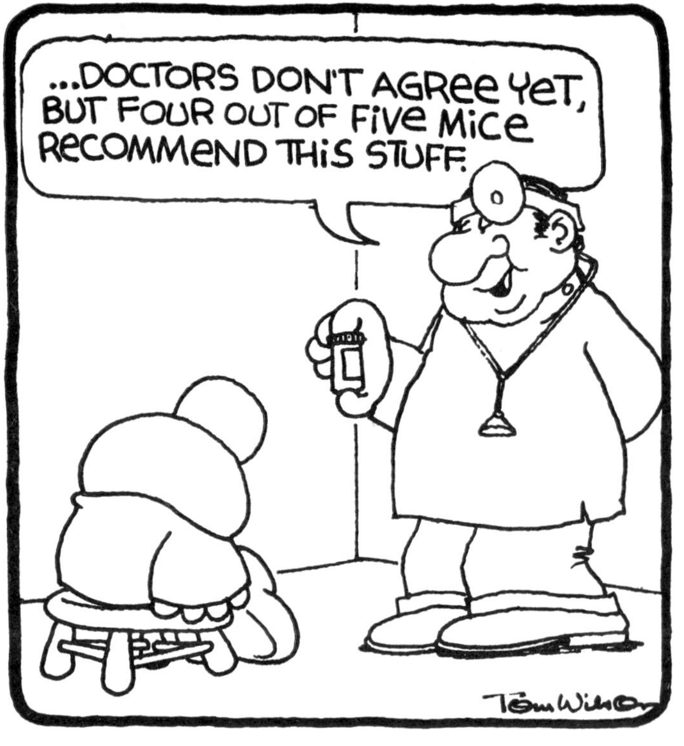
...DOCTORS DON'T AGREE YET, BUT FOUR OUT OF FIVE MICE RECOMMEND THIS STUFF.
Tom Wilson

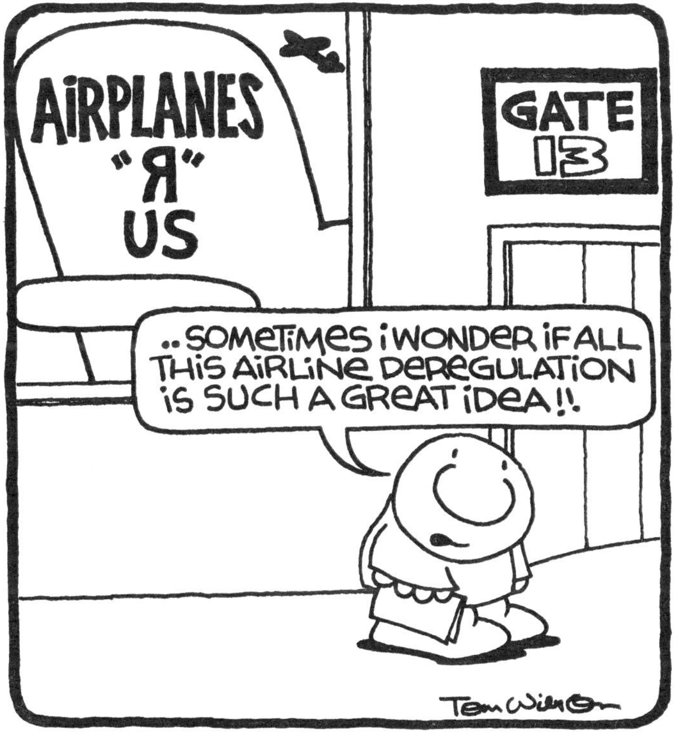
AIRPLANES "R" US
GATE 13
..SOMETIMES I WONDER IF ALL THIS AIRLINE DEREGULATION IS SUCH A GREAT IDEA!!.
Tom Wilson

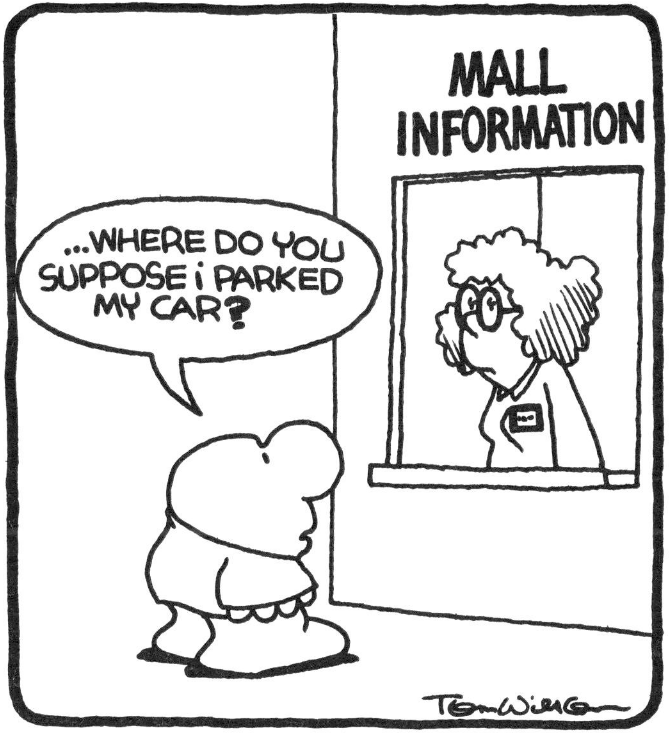
MALL INFORMATION
...WHERE DO YOU SUPPOSE I PARKED MY CAR?
Tom Wilson

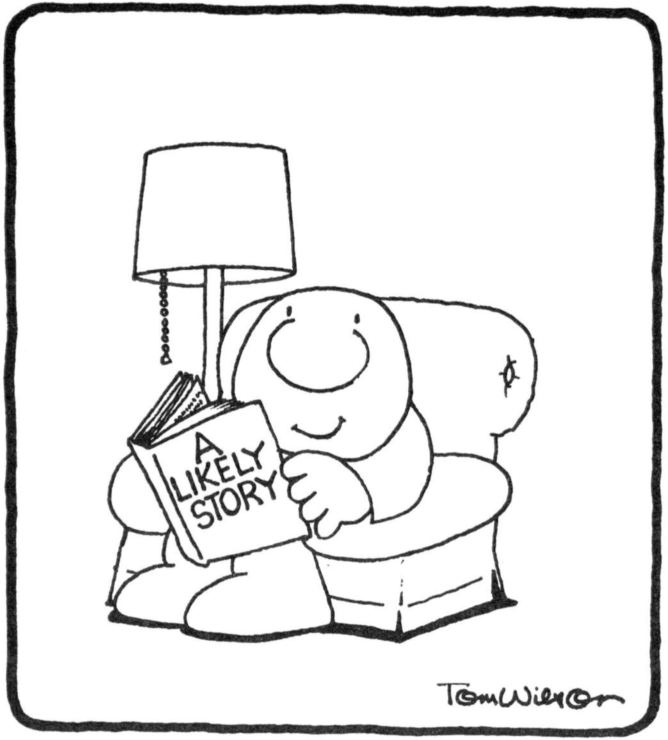
A
LIKELY
STORY
Tom Wilson

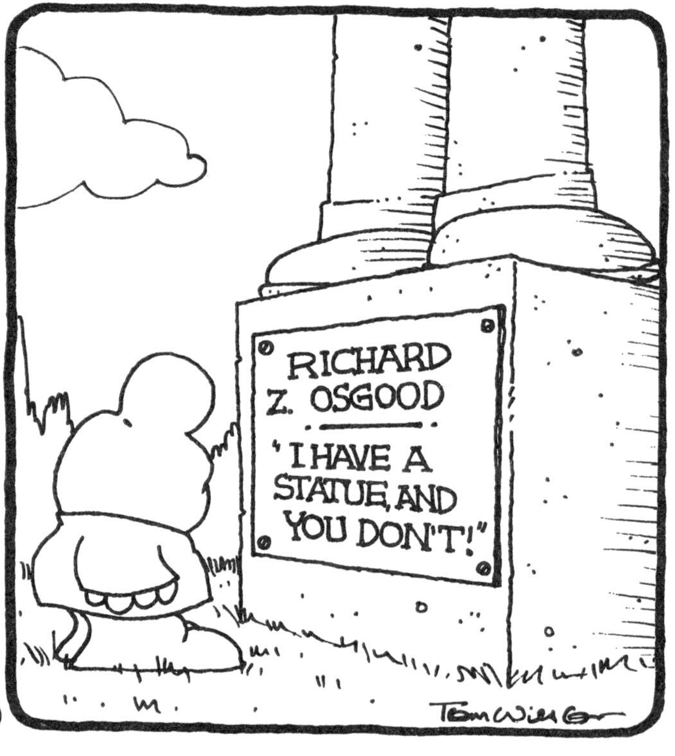
RICHARD
Z. OSGOOD
"I HAVE A
STATUE, AND
YOU DON'T!"
Tom Wilson

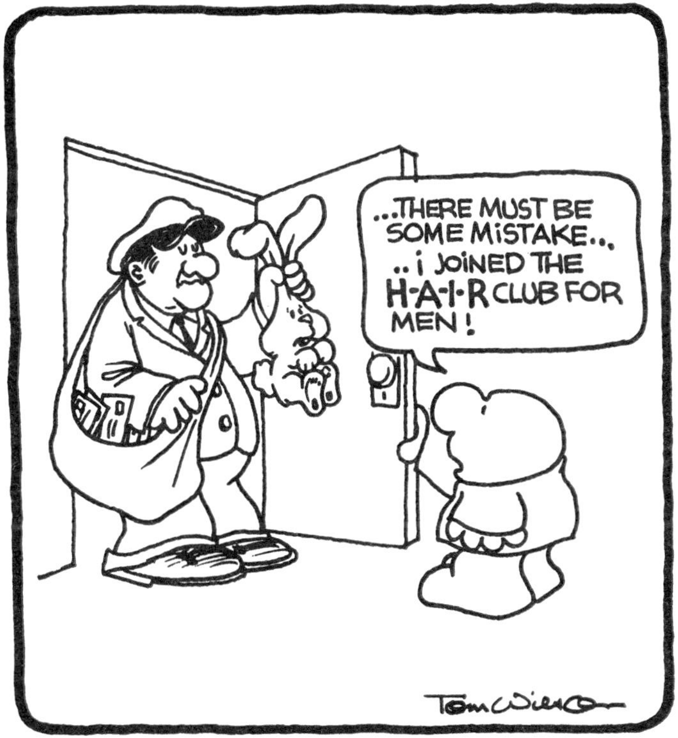
...THERE MUST BE SOME MiSTAKE... ..i JOINED THE H-A-I-R CLUB FOR MEN!
Tom Wilson

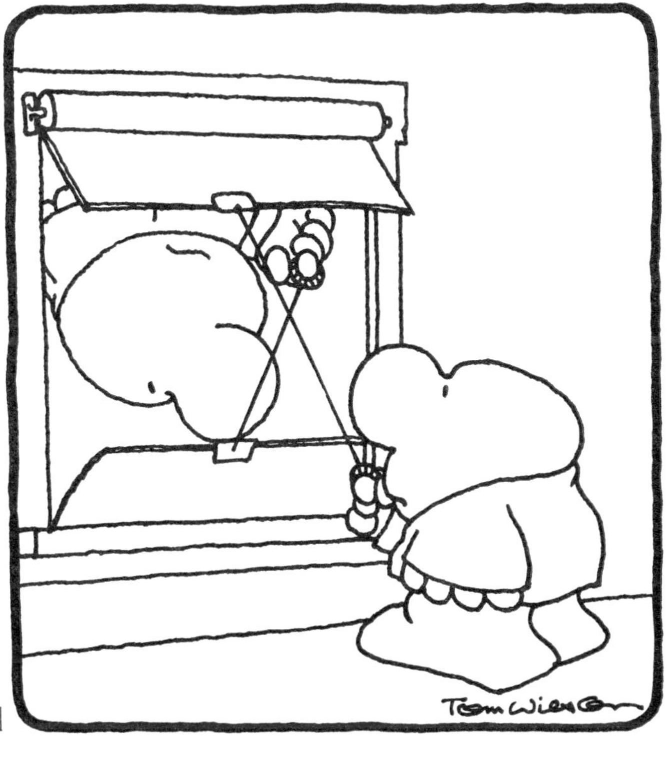
Tom Wilson

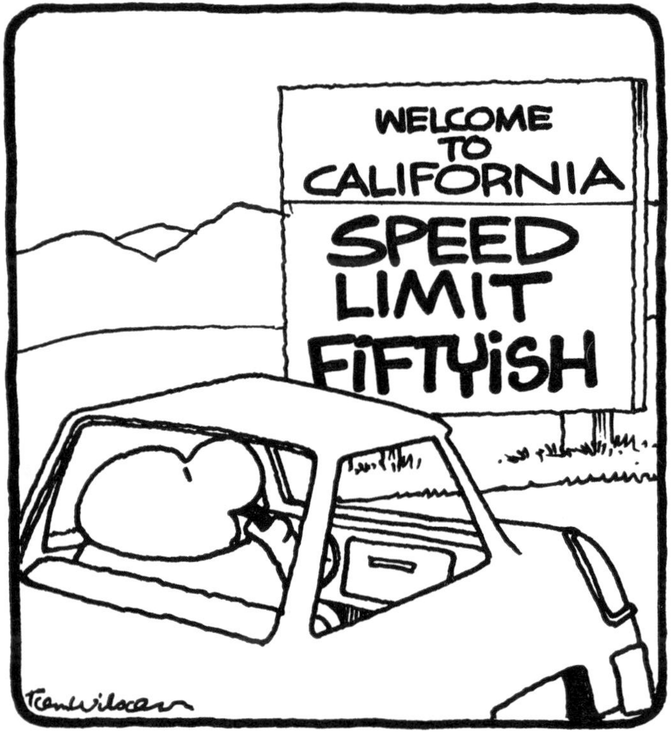
WELCOME
TO
CALIFORNIA
SPEED
LIMIT
FIFTYISH
Tom Wilson

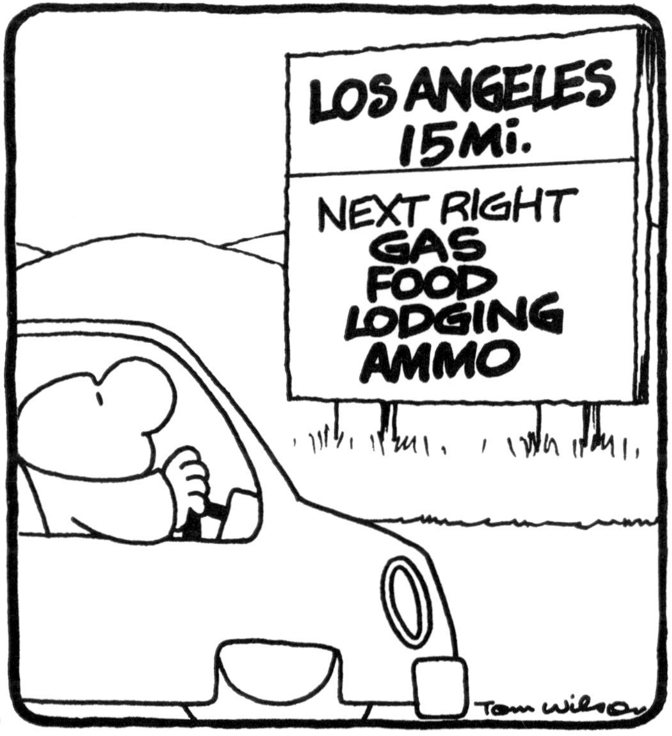
LOS ANGELES
15 Mi.
NEXT RIGHT
GAS
FOOD
LODGING
AMMO
Tom Wilson

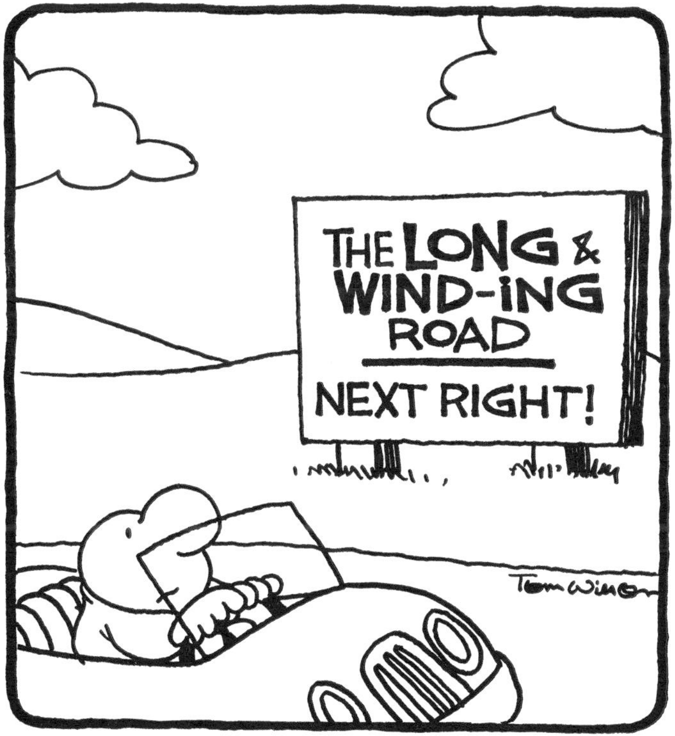
THE LONG & WIND-ING ROAD
NEXT RIGHT!
Tom Wilson

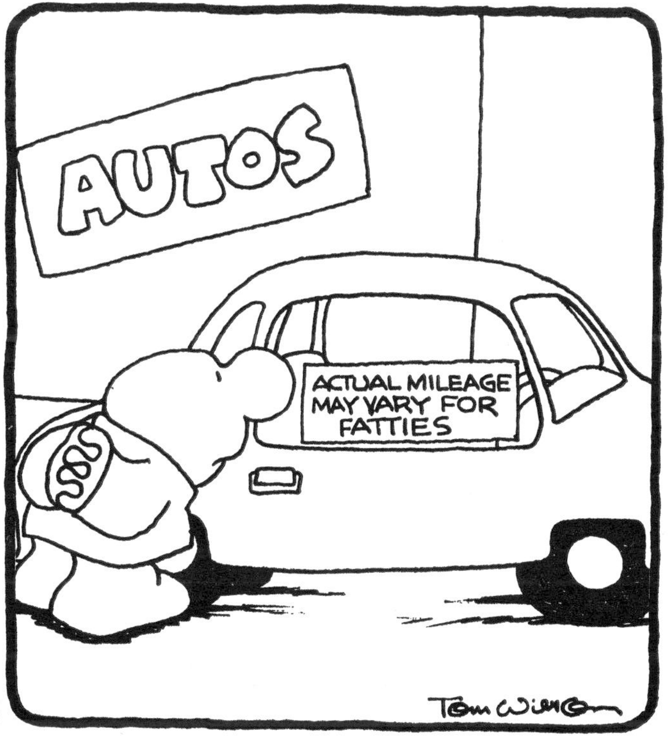
AUTOS
ACTUAL MILEAGE MAY VARY FOR FATTIES
Tom Wilson

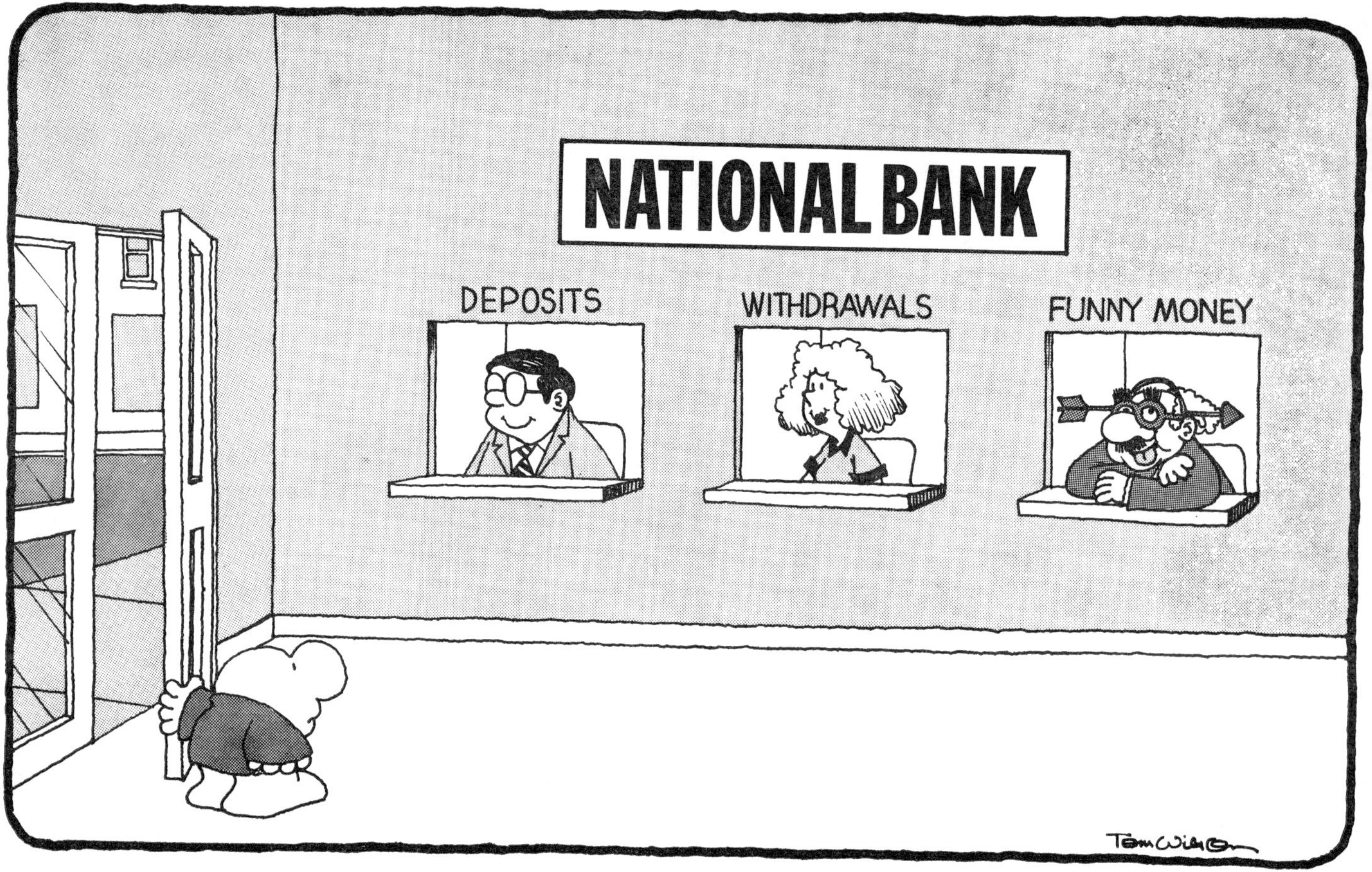
NATIONAL BANK
DEPOSITS
WITHDRAWALS
FUNNY MONEY
Tom Wilson

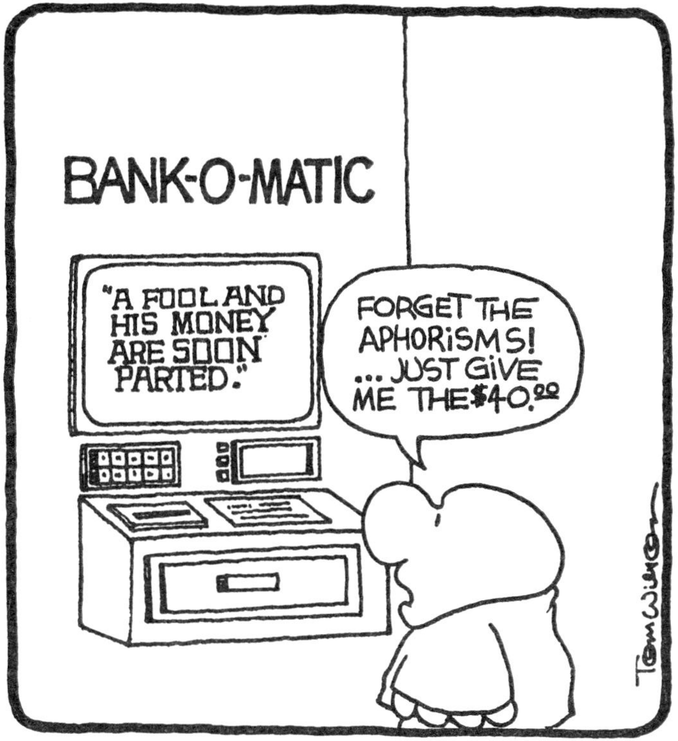
BANK-O-MATIC
"A FOOL AND HIS MONEY ARE SOON PARTED."
FORGET THE APHORISMS! ... JUST GIVE ME THE $40.00
Tom Wilson

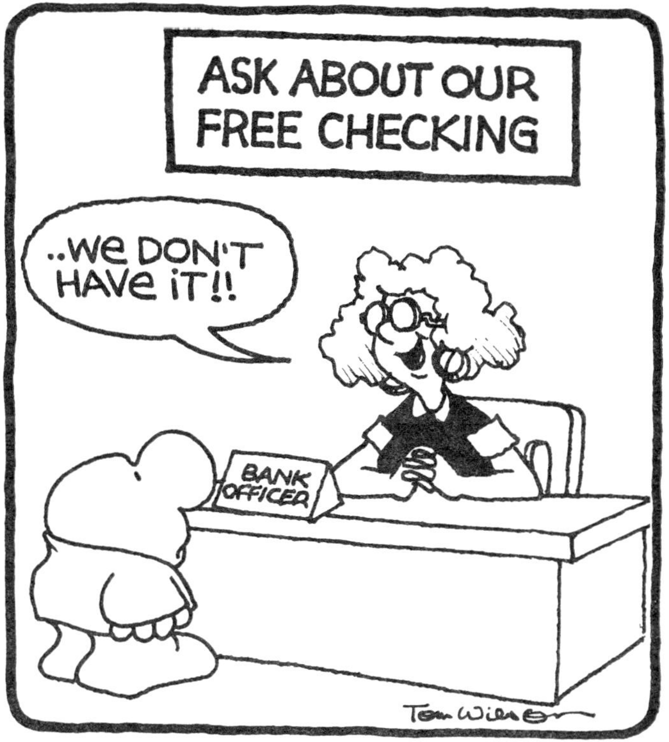
ASK ABOUT OUR FREE CHECKING
..WE DON'T HAVE IT!!
BANK OFFICER
Tom Wilson

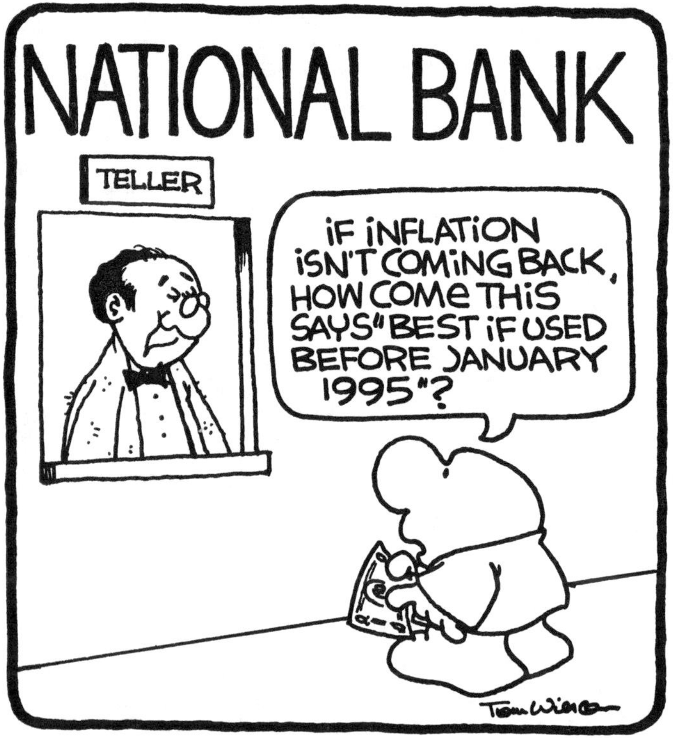
NATIONAL BANK
TELLER
IF INFLATION ISN'T COMING BACK, HOW COME THIS SAYS "BEST IF USED BEFORE JANUARY 1995"?
Tom Wilson

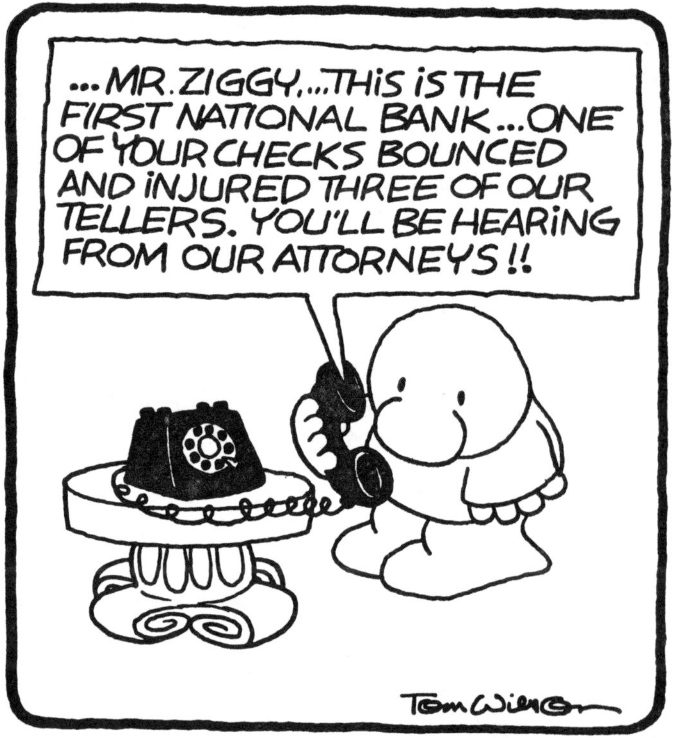
...MR. ZIGGY,...THIS IS THE FIRST NATIONAL BANK...ONE OF YOUR CHECKS BOUNCED AND INJURED THREE OF OUR TELLERS. YOU'LL BE HEARING FROM OUR ATTORNEYS!!
Tom Wilson

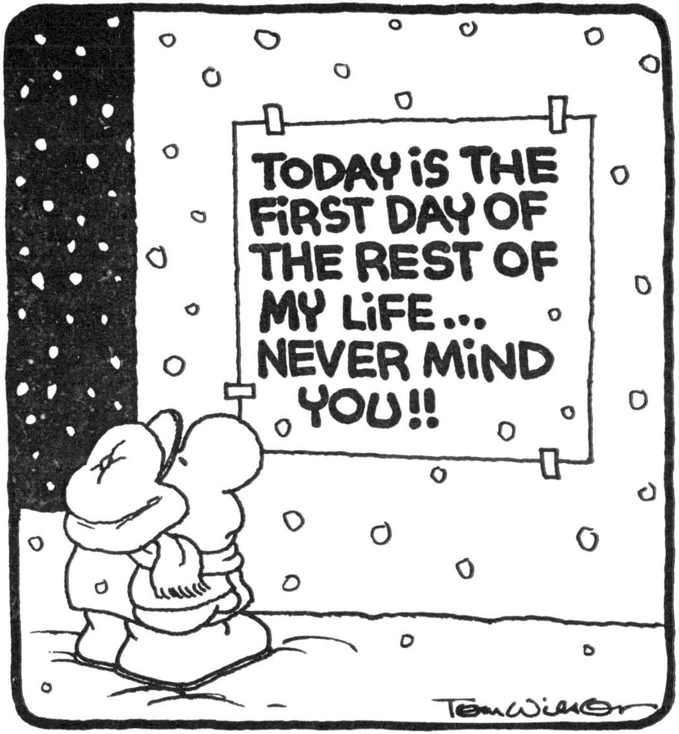
TODAY IS THE FIRST DAY OF THE REST OF MY LIFE... NEVER MIND YOU!!

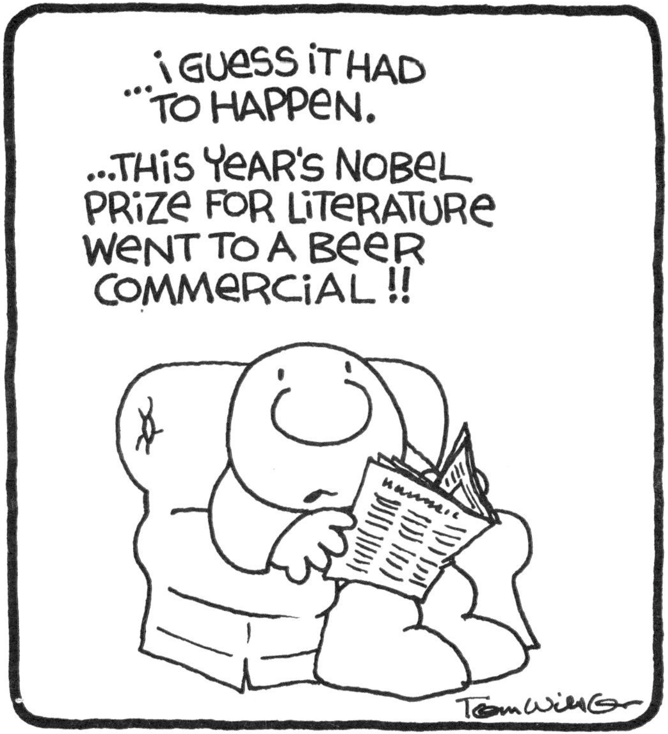
...I GUESS IT HAD TO HAPPEN.
...THIS YEAR'S NOBEL PRIZE FOR LITERATURE WENT TO A BEER COMMERCIAL!!

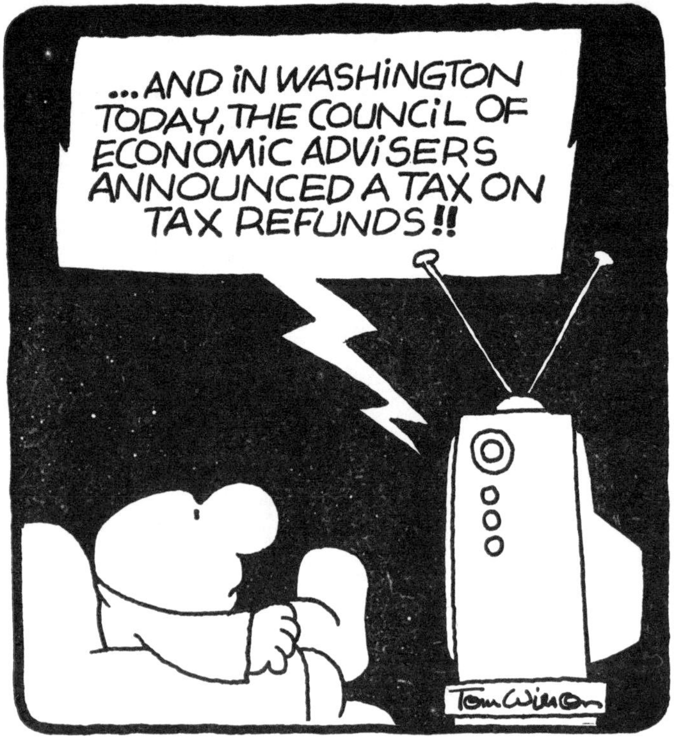
...AND IN WASHINGTON TODAY, THE COUNCIL OF ECONOMIC ADVISERS ANNOUNCED A TAX ON TAX REFUNDS!!
Tom Wilson

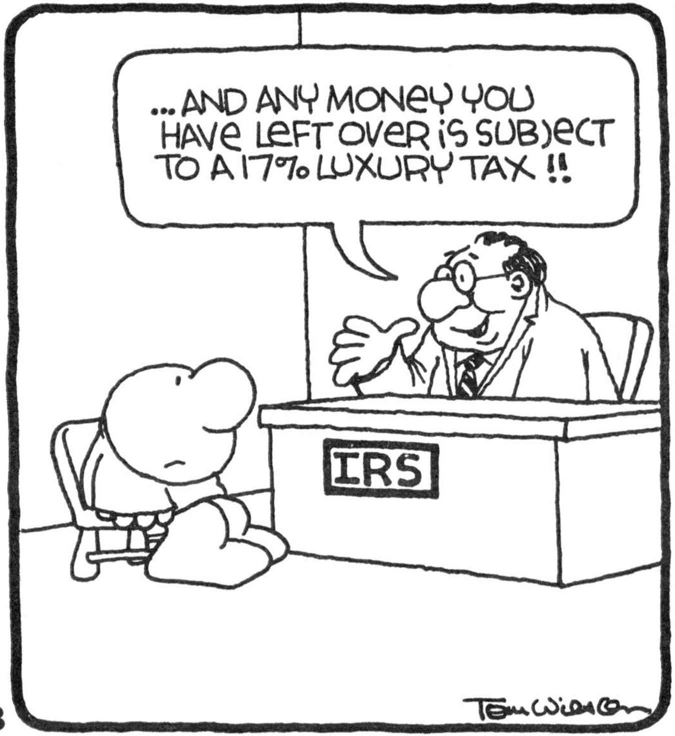
...AND ANY MONEY YOU HAVE LEFT OVER IS SUBJECT TO A 17% LUXURY TAX!!
IRS
Tom Wilson

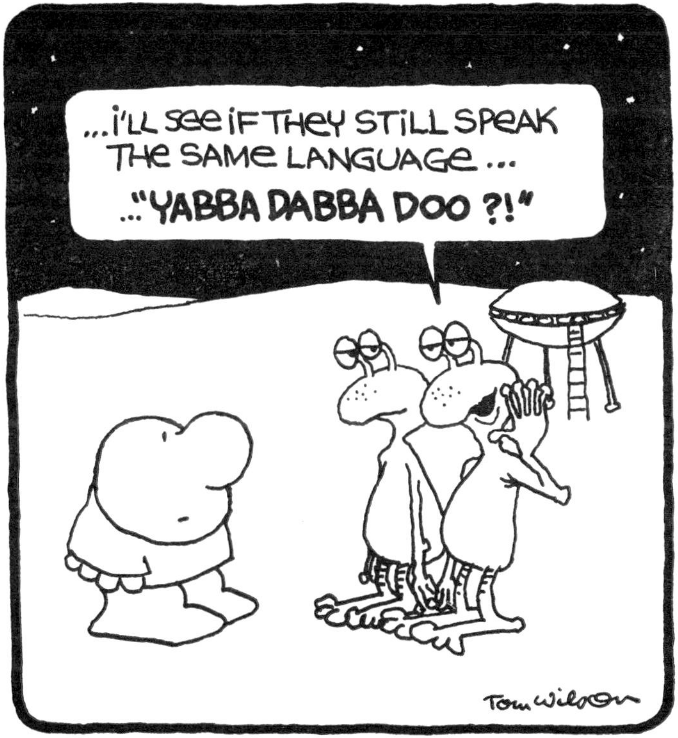
...I'LL SEE IF THEY STILL SPEAK THE SAME LANGUAGE ...
..."YABBA DABBA DOO ?!"
Tom Wilson

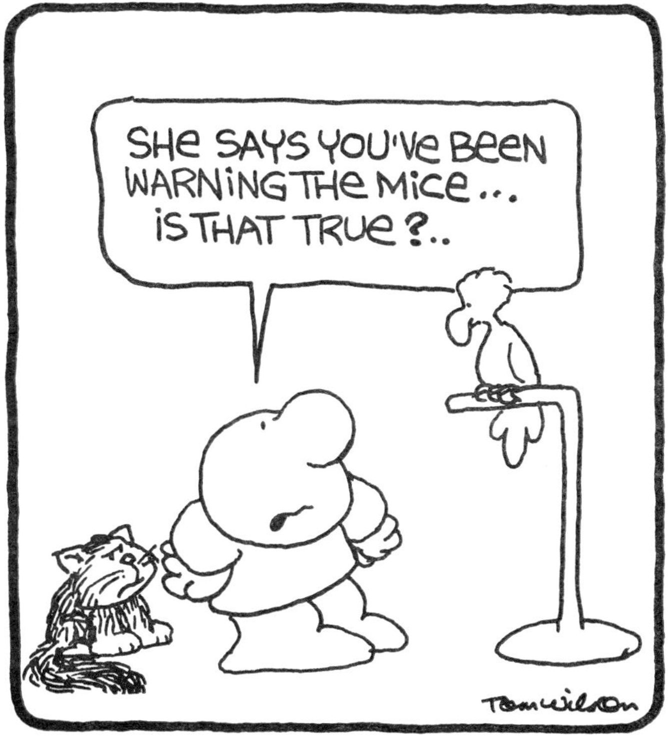
SHE SAYS YOU'VE BEEN WARNING THE MICE ... IS THAT TRUE ?..
Tom Wilson

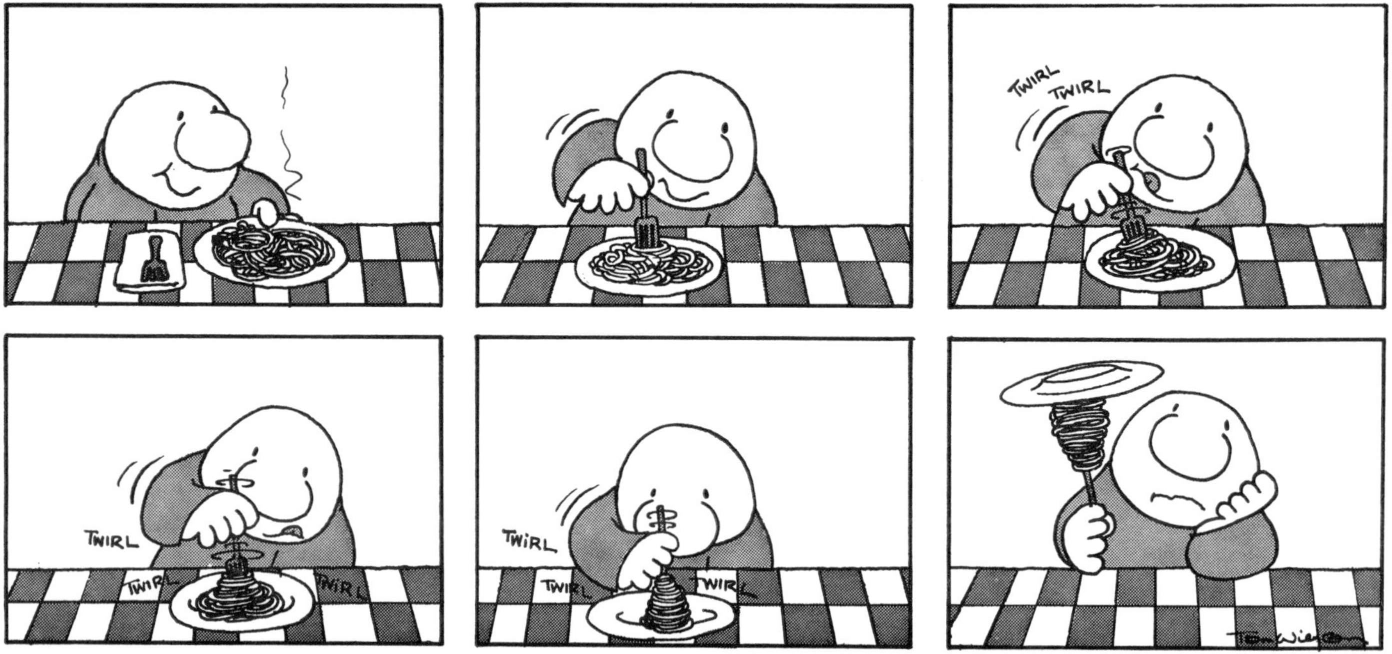
TWIRL
TWIRL
TWIRL
TWIRL
TWIRL
TWIRL
TWIRL
TWIRL

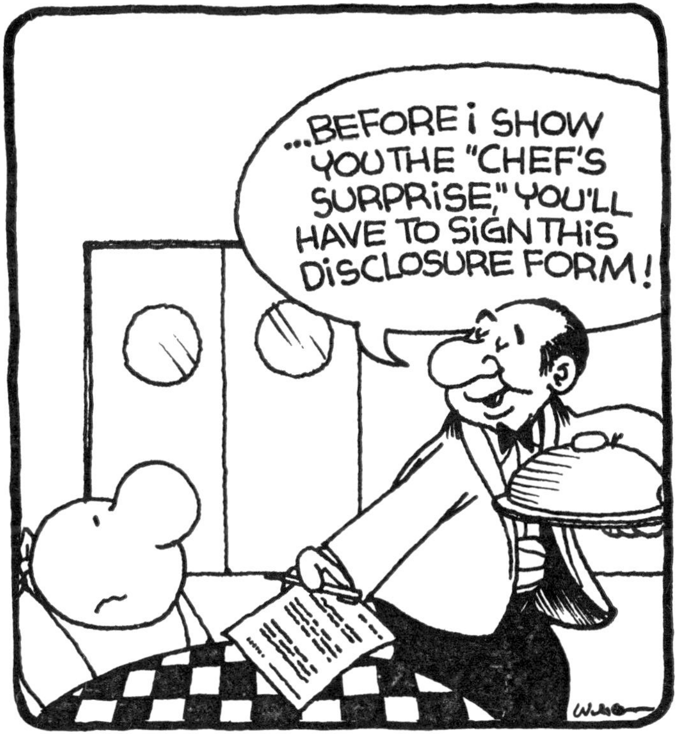
...BEFORE i SHOW YOU THE "CHEF'S SURPRISE," YOU'LL HAVE TO SIGN THIS DISCLOSURE FORM!

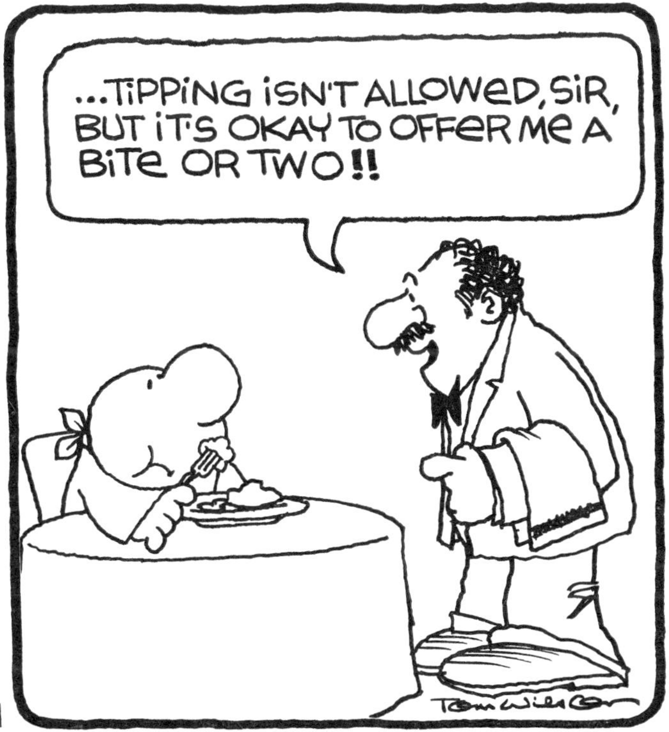
...TIPPING ISN'T ALLOWED, SIR, BUT IT'S OKAY TO OFFER ME A BITE OR TWO!!
Tom Wilson

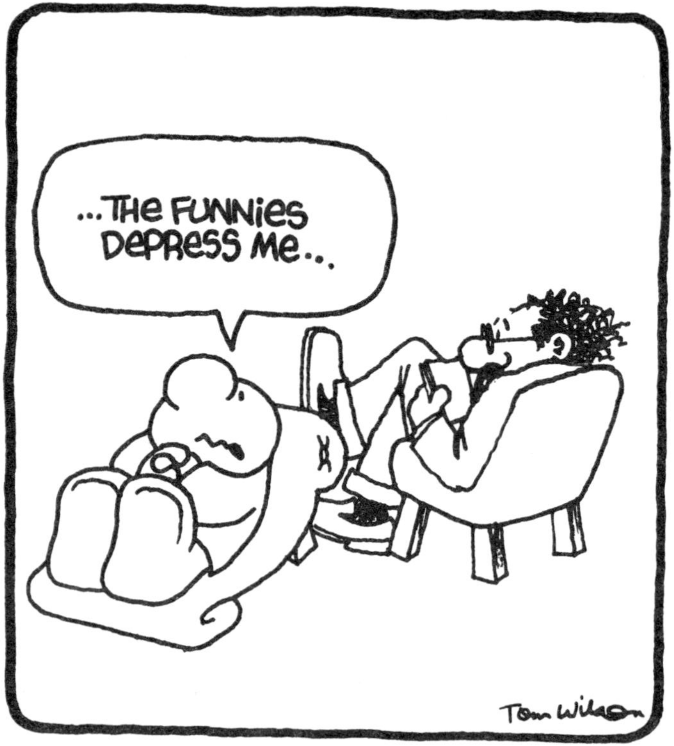
...THE FUNNIES DEPRESS ME...
Tom Wilson

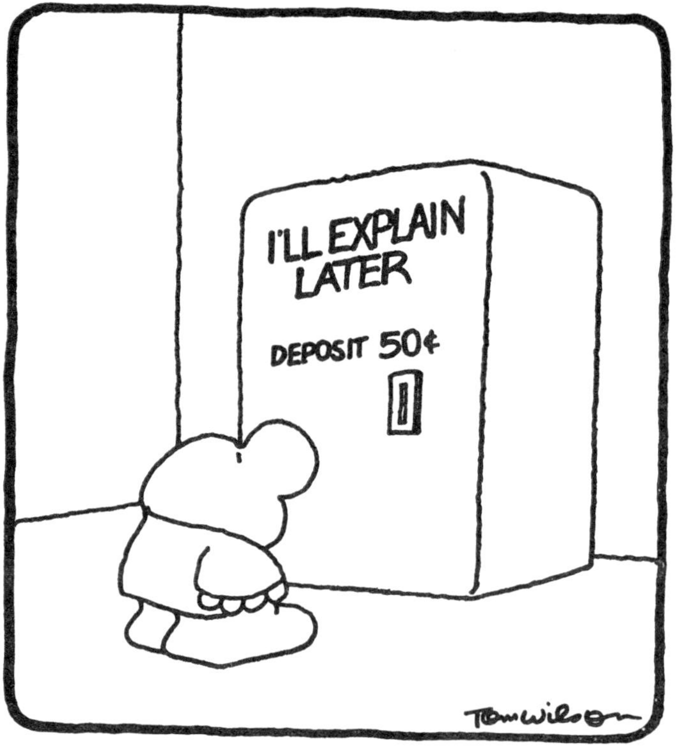
I'LL EXPLAIN LATER
DEPOSIT 50¢
Tom Wilson

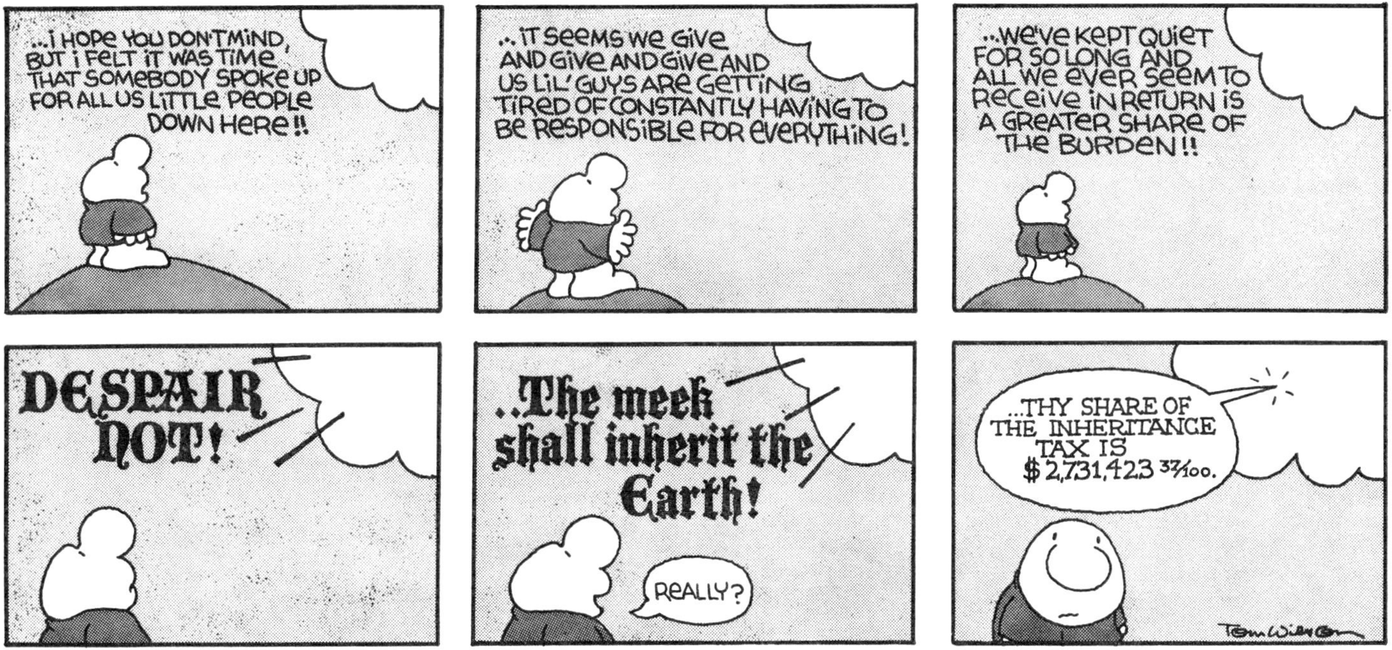
...i HOPE YOU DON'T MIND, BUT i FELT iT WAS TiME THAT SOMEBODY SPOKE UP FOR ALL US LiTTLE PEOPLE DOWN HERE!!
.. iT SEEMS WE GiVE AND GiVE AND GiVE AND US LiL' GUYS ARE GETTiNG TiRED OF CONSTANTLY HAViNG TO BE RESPONSiBLE FOR EVERYTHiNG!
...WE'VE KEPT QUiET FOR SO LONG AND ALL WE EVER SEEM TO RECEiVE iN RETURN iS A GREATER SHARE OF THE BURDEN!!
DESPAIR NOT!
..The meek shall inherit the Earth!
REALLY?
...THY SHARE OF THE INHERITANCE TAX IS $2,731,423 33/100.
Tom Wilson

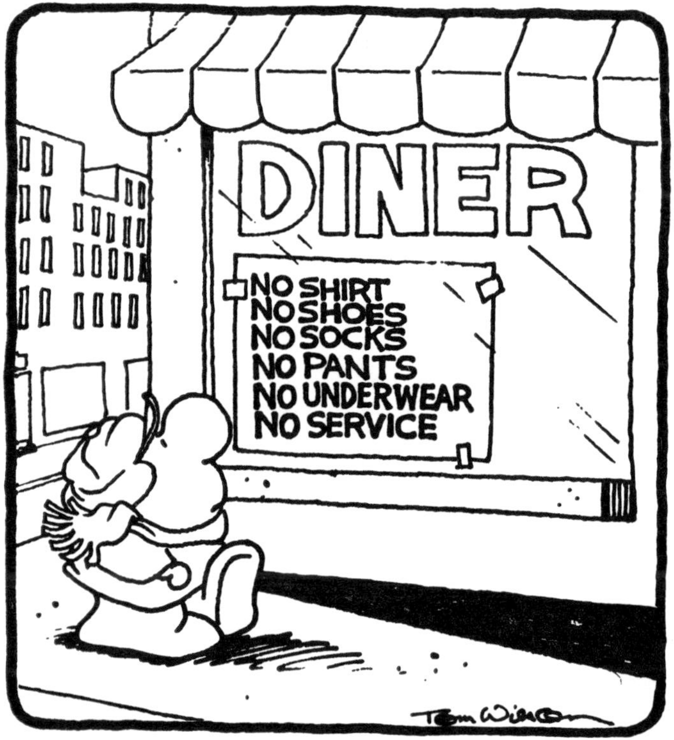
DINER
NO SHIRT
NO SHOES
NO SOCKS
NO PANTS
NO UNDERWEAR
NO SERVICE

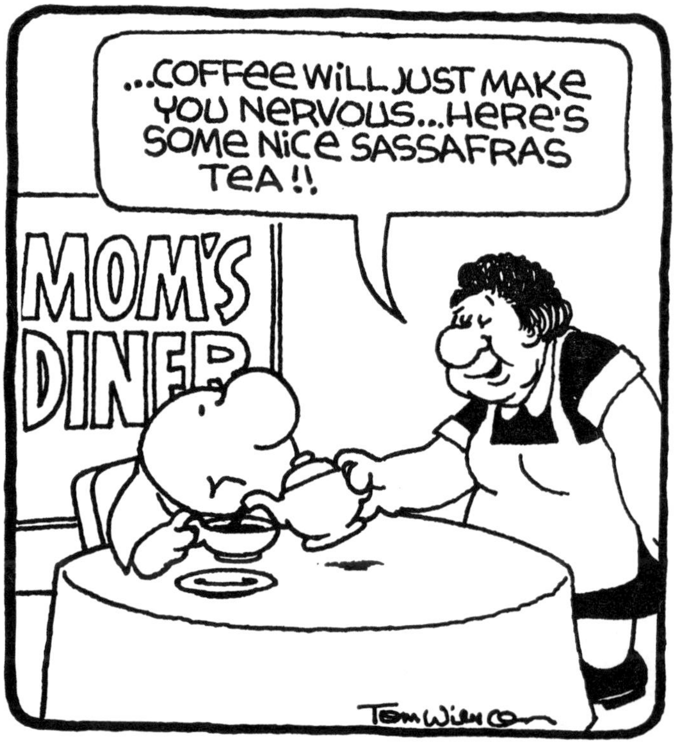
...COFFEE WILL JUST MAKE YOU NERVOUS...HERE'S SOME NICE SASSAFRAS TEA!!
MOM'S DINER

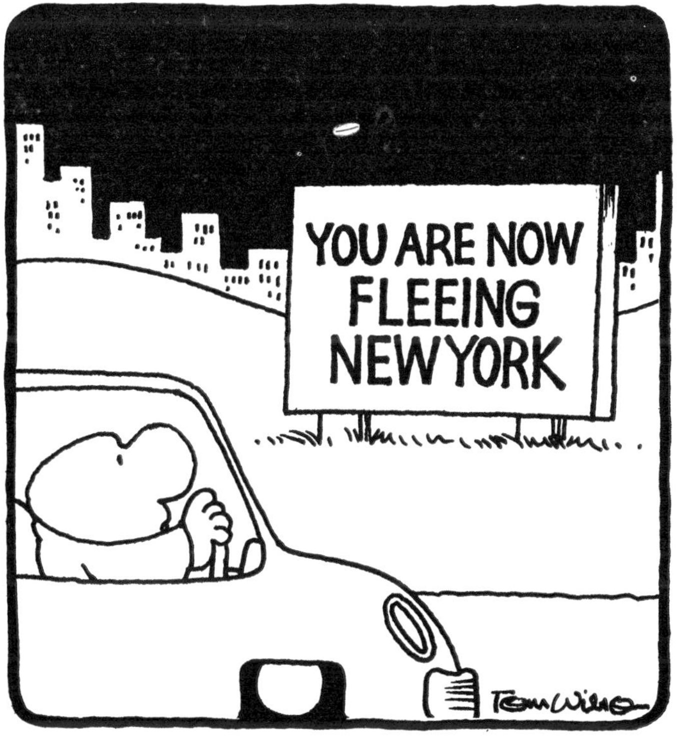
YOU ARE NOW FLEEING NEW YORK
TOM WILSON

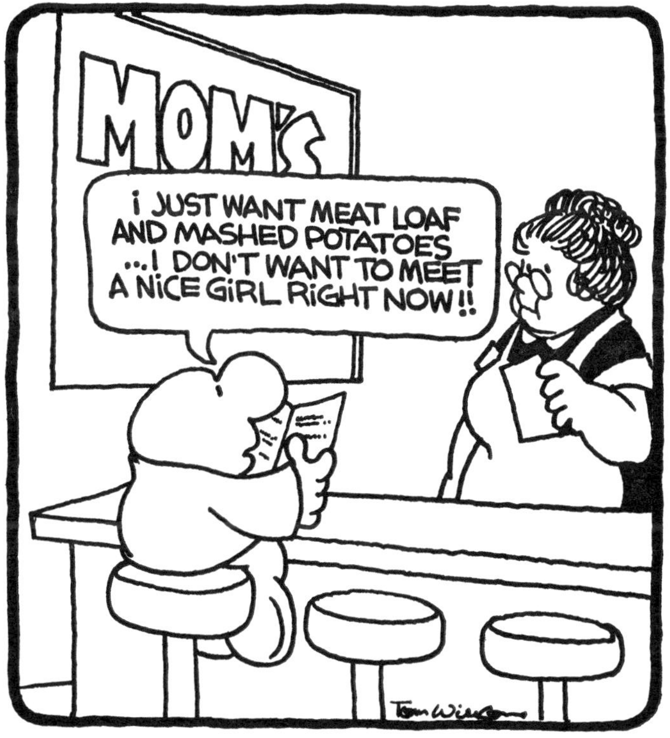
MOM'S
I JUST WANT MEAT LOAF AND MASHED POTATOES ...I DON'T WANT TO MEET A NICE GIRL RIGHT NOW!!
TOM WILSON

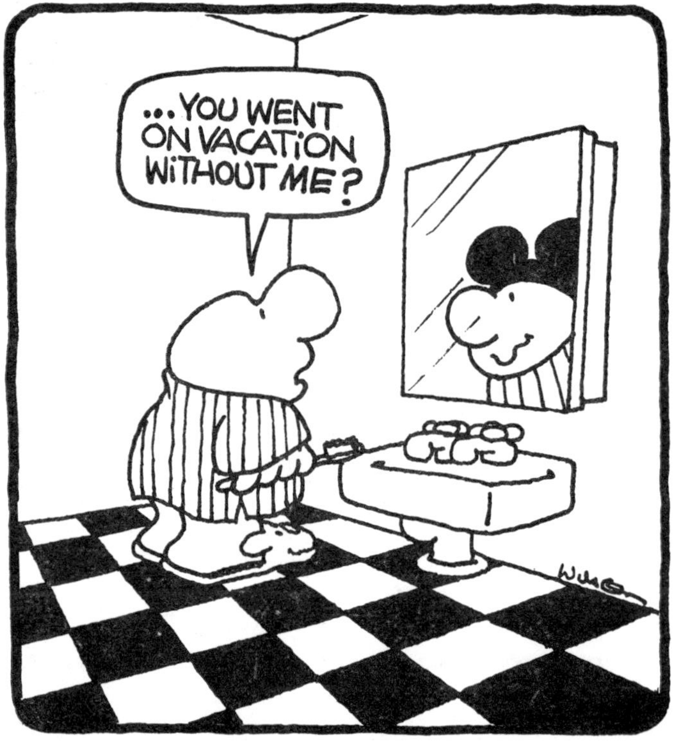
...YOU WENT ON VACATION WITHOUT ME?
WILSON

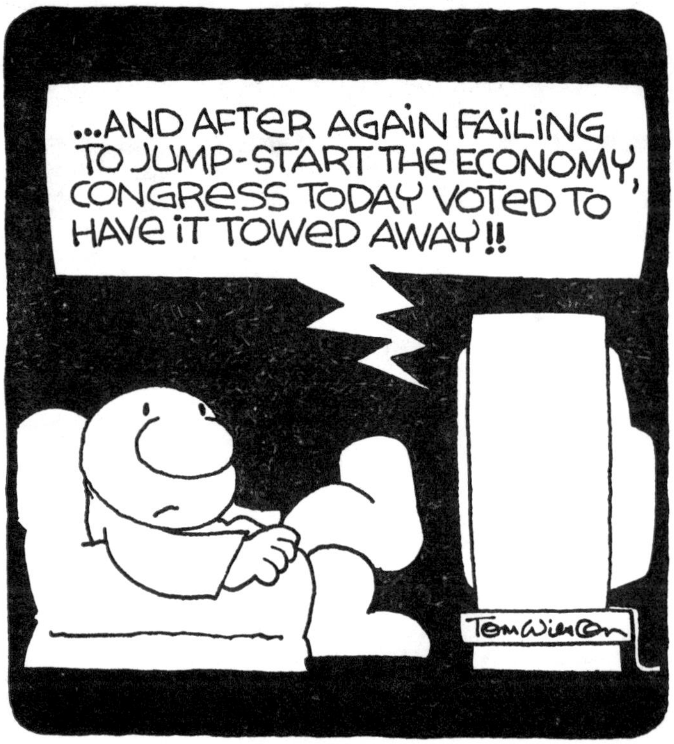
...AND AFTER AGAIN FAILING TO JUMP-START THE ECONOMY, CONGRESS TODAY VOTED TO HAVE IT TOWED AWAY!!
TOM WILSON

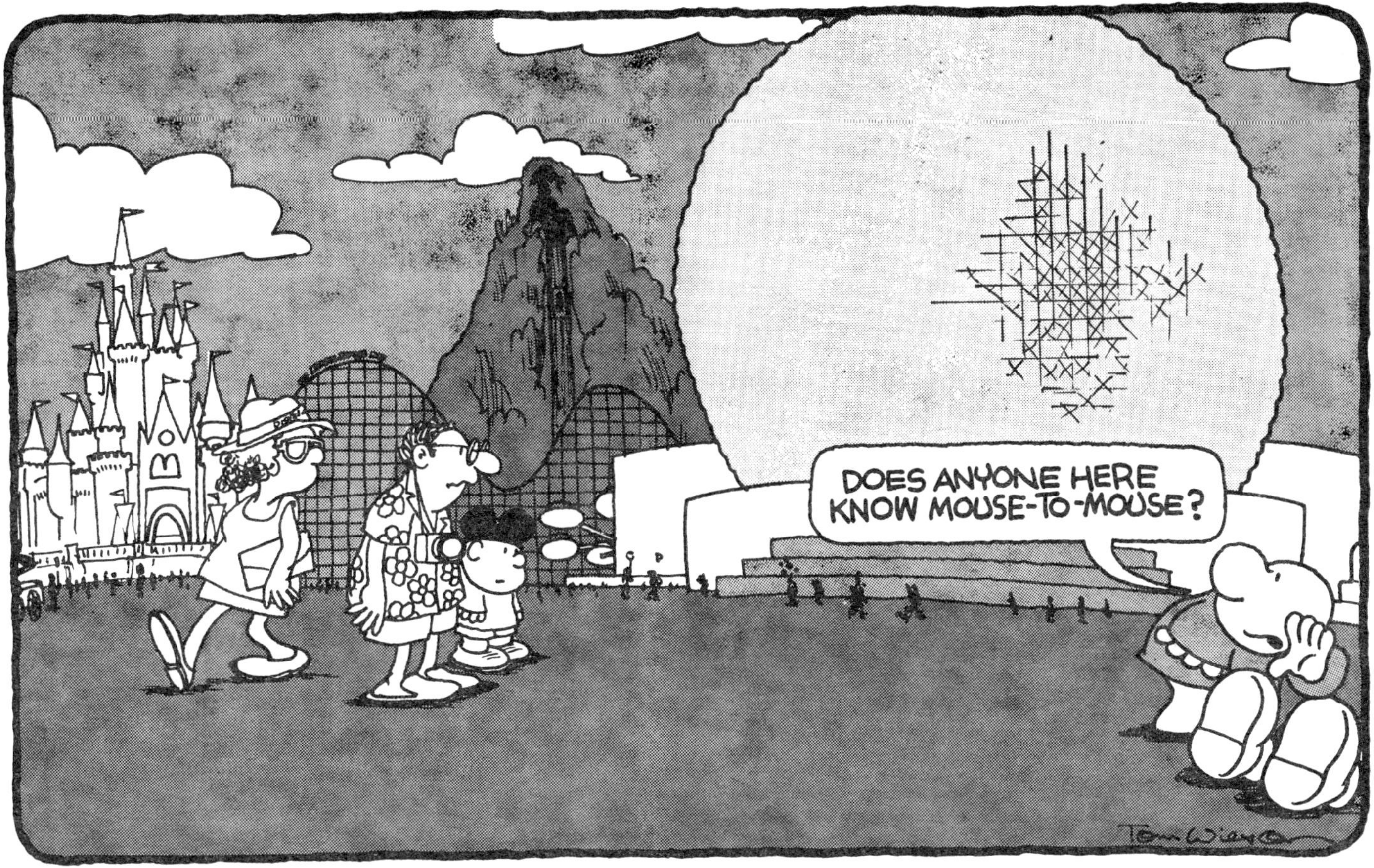
DOES ANYONE HERE KNOW MOUSE-TO-MOUSE?

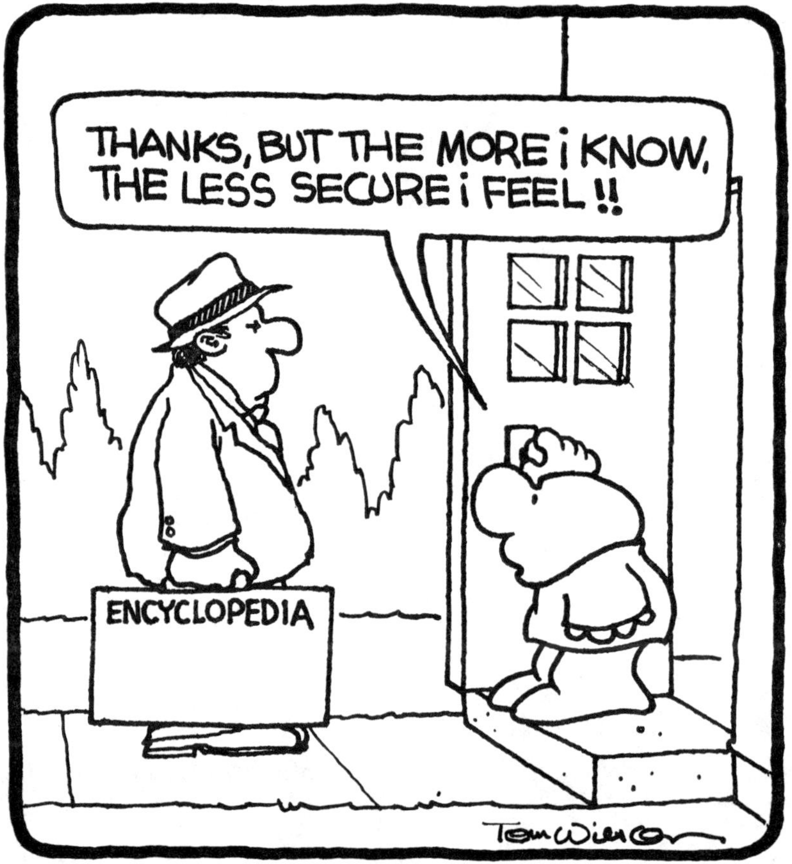
THANKS, BUT THE MORE i KNOW, THE LESS SECURE i FEEL !!
ENCYCLOPEDIA
Tom Wilson

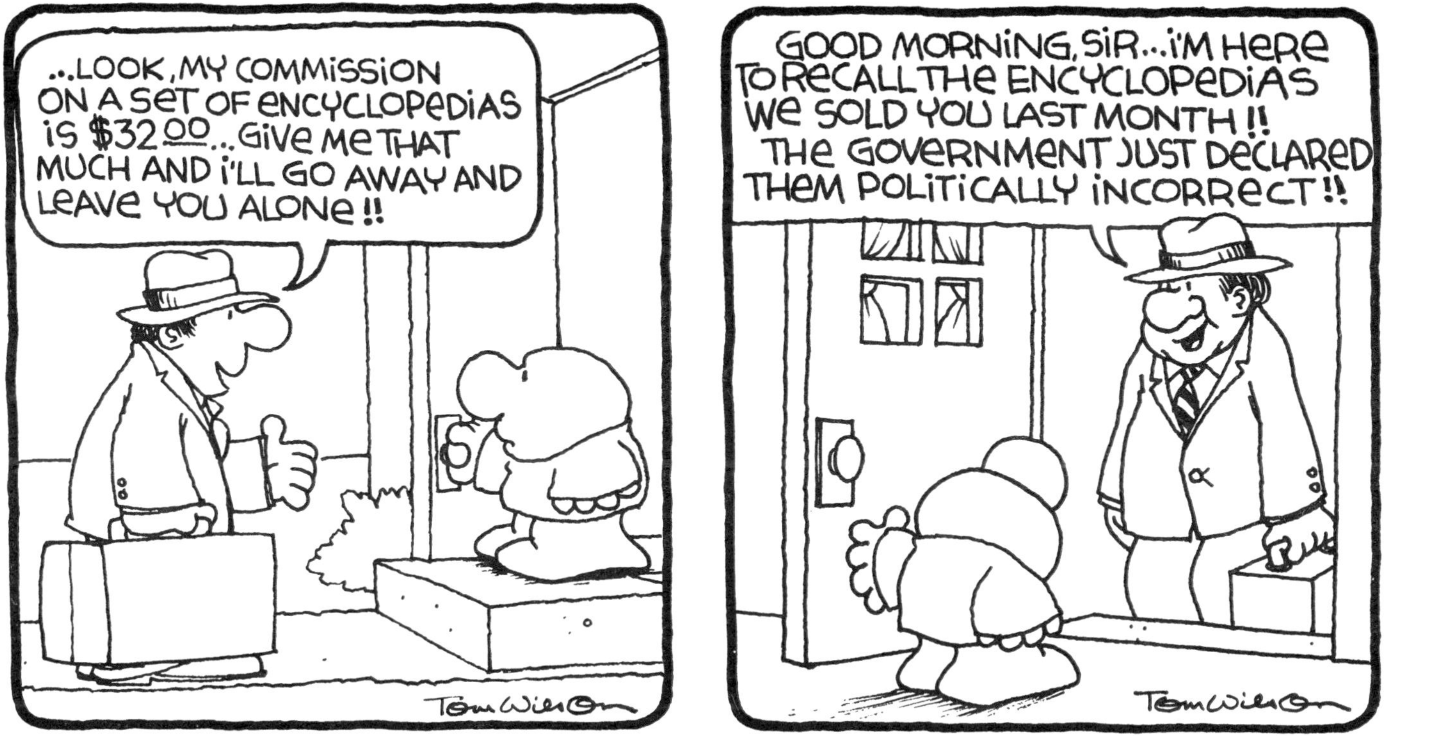
...LOOK, MY COMMISSION ON A SET OF ENCYCLOPEDIAS IS $32.00... GIVE ME THAT MUCH AND I'LL GO AWAY AND LEAVE YOU ALONE!!
Tom Wilson
GOOD MORNING, SIR... I'M HERE TO RECALL THE ENCYCLOPEDIAS WE SOLD YOU LAST MONTH!! THE GOVERNMENT JUST DECLARED THEM POLITICALLY INCORRECT!!
Tom Wilson

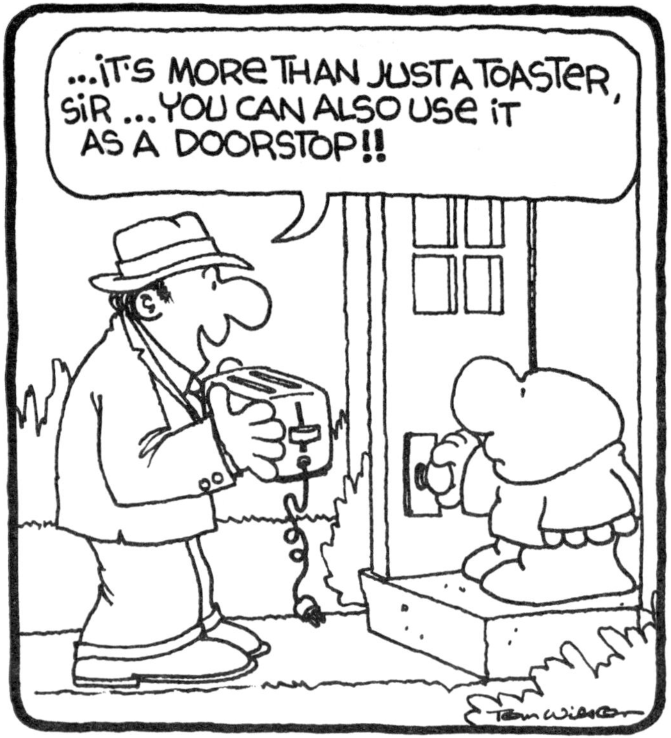
...IT'S MORE THAN JUST A TOASTER, SIR ... YOU CAN ALSO USE IT AS A DOORSTOP!!
Tom Wilson

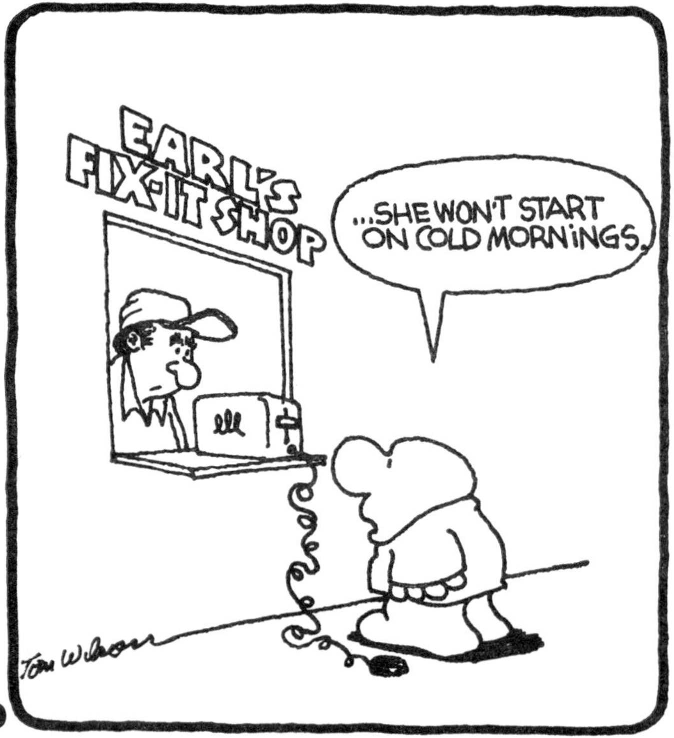
EARL'S FIX-IT SHOP
...SHE WON'T START ON COLD MORNINGS.
Tom Wilson

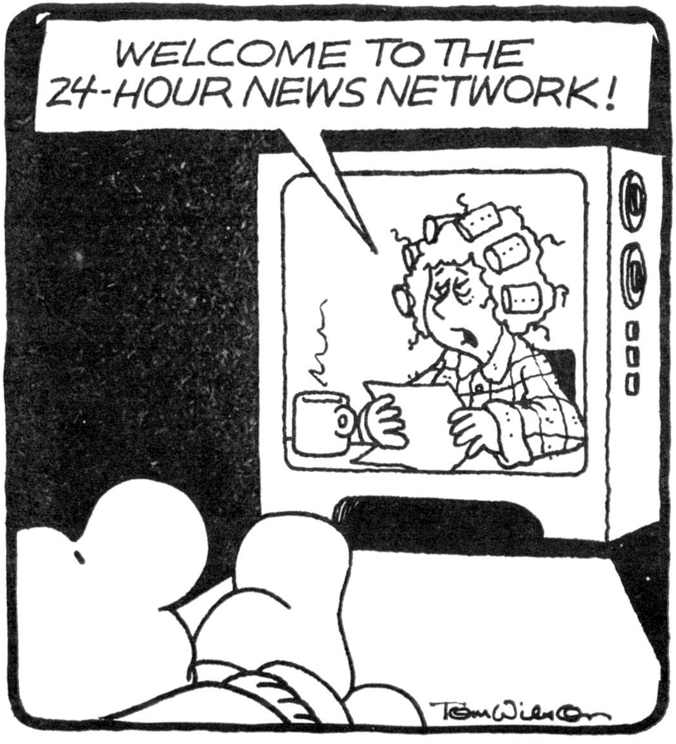
WELCOME TO THE 24-HOUR NEWS NETWORK!
TOM WILSON

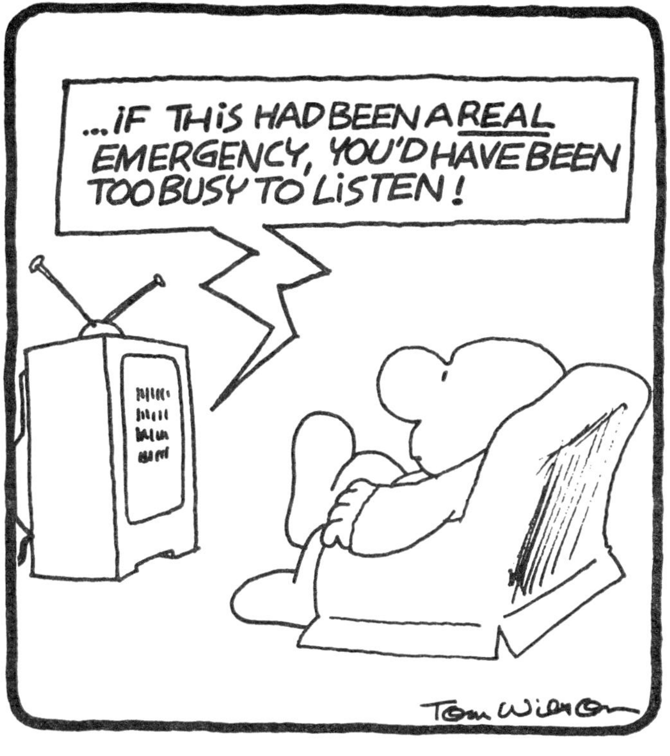
...IF THIS HAD BEEN A REAL EMERGENCY, YOU'D HAVE BEEN TOO BUSY TO LISTEN!
TOM WILSON

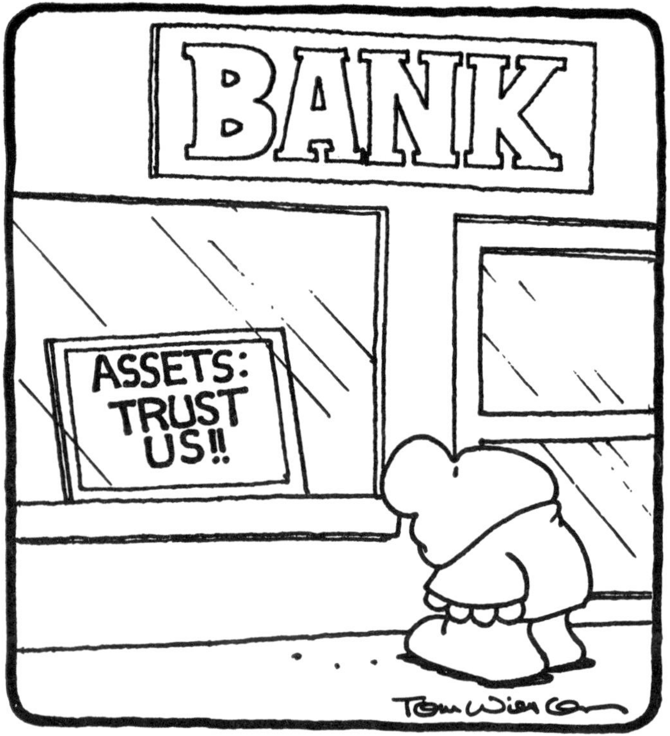
BANK
ASSETS: TRUST US!!
Tom Wilson

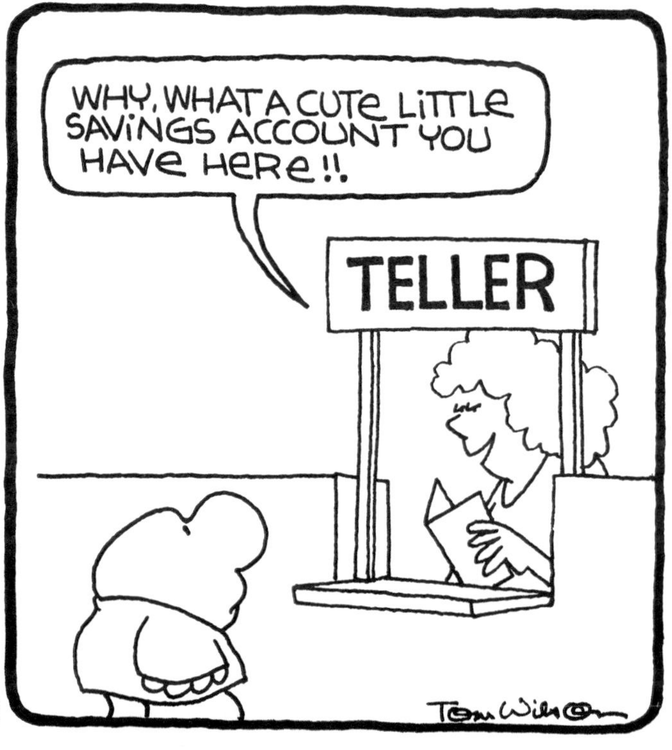
WHY, WHAT A CUTE LITTLE SAVINGS ACCOUNT YOU HAVE HERE!!
TELLER
Tom Wilson

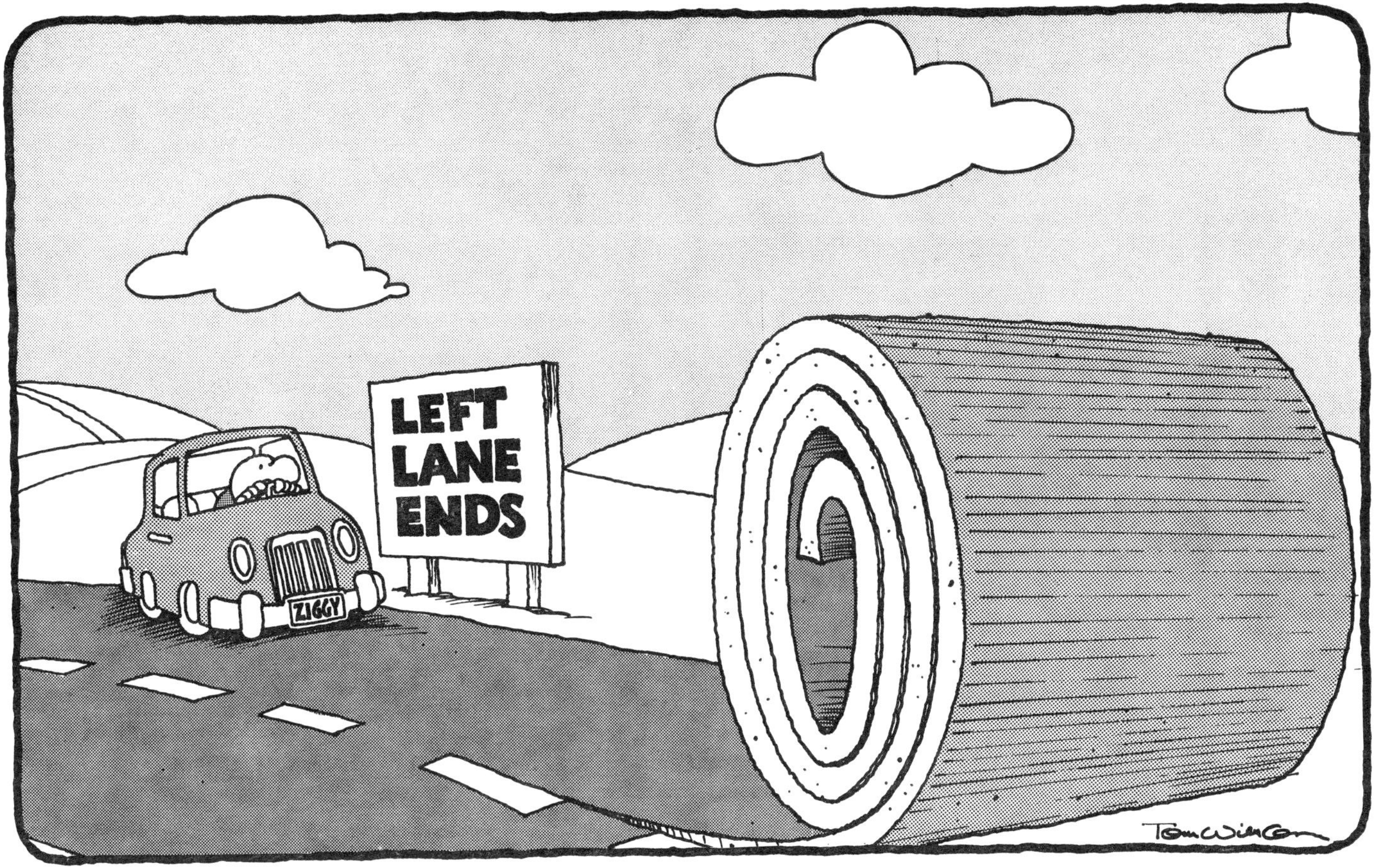
LEFT LANE ENDS
ZIGGY
Tom Wilson

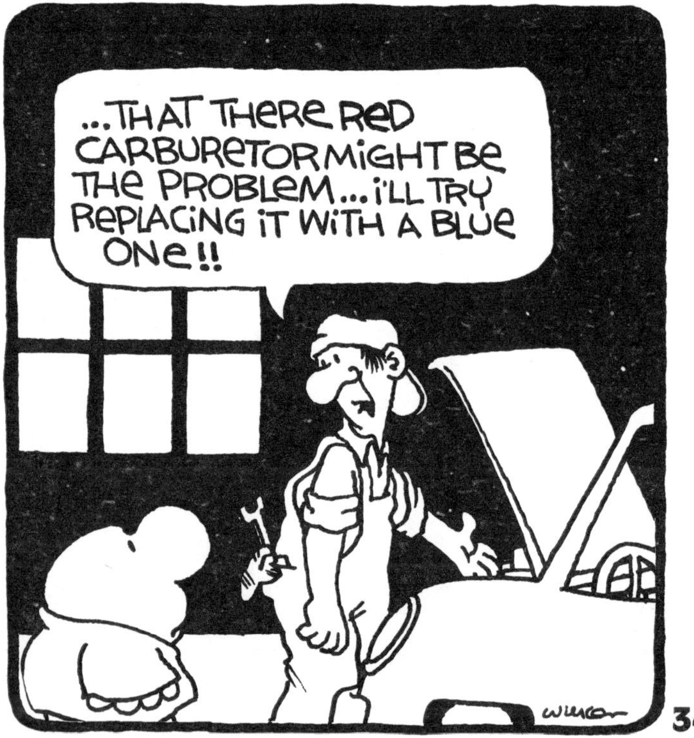
...THAT THERE RED CARBURETOR MIGHT BE THE PROBLEM... I'LL TRY REPLACING IT WITH A BLUE ONE !!
WILSON

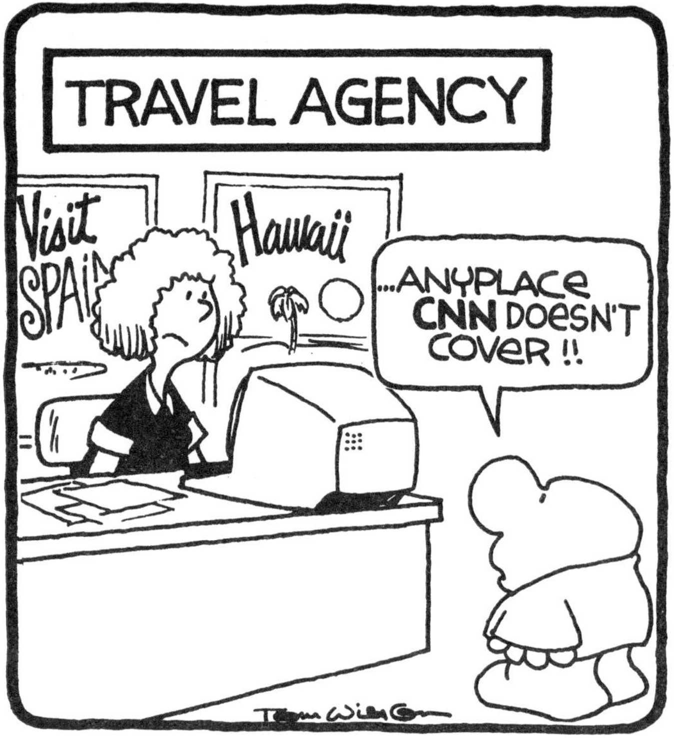
TRAVEL AGENCY
Visit SPAI
Hawaii
...ANYPLACE CNN DOESN'T COVER !!
TOM WILSON

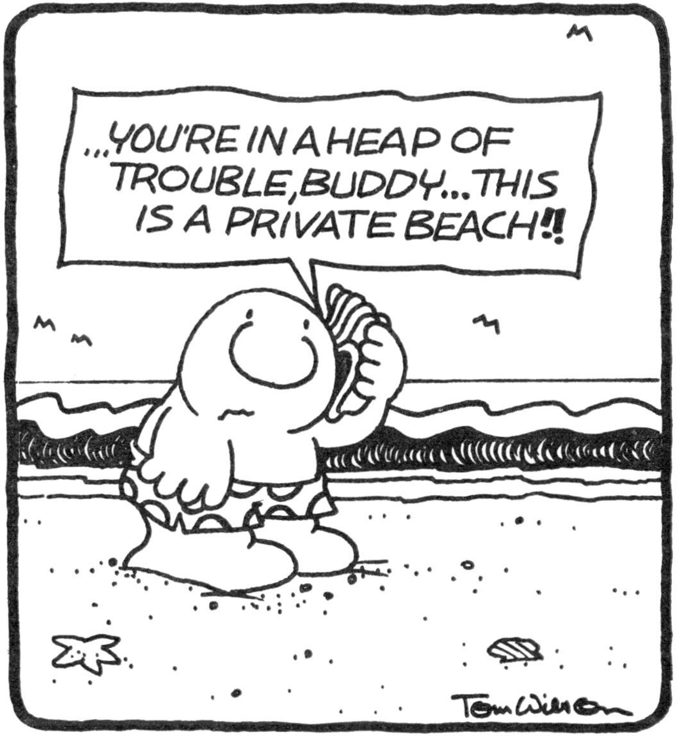
...YOU'RE IN A HEAP OF TROUBLE, BUDDY... THIS IS A PRIVATE BEACH!!
Tom Wilson

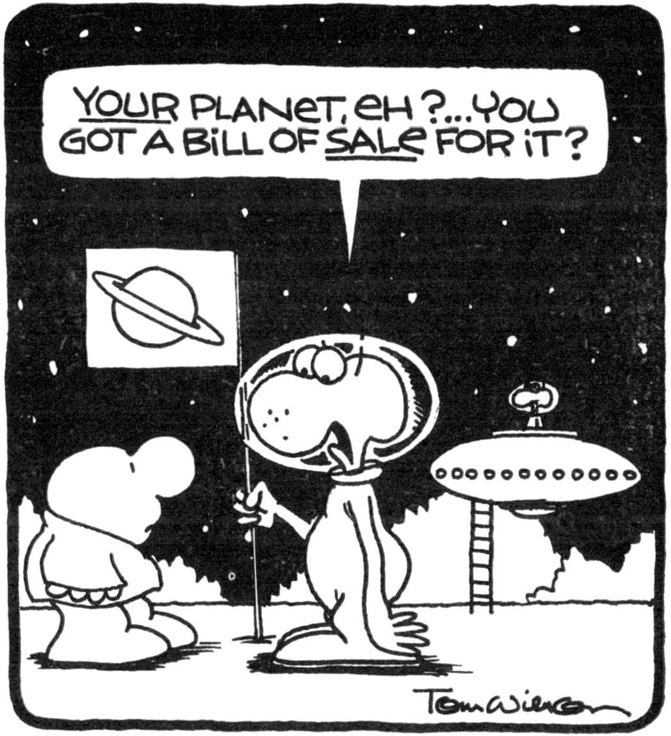
YOUR PLANET, EH?... YOU GOT A BILL OF SALE FOR IT?
Tom Wilson

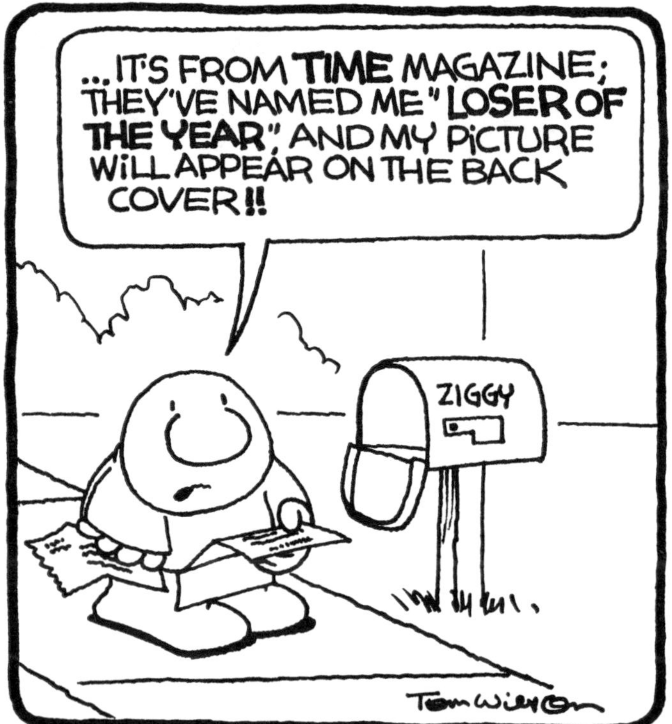
...IT'S FROM **TIME** MAGAZINE; THEY'VE NAMED ME "**LOSER OF THE YEAR**," AND MY PICTURE WILL APPEAR ON THE BACK COVER!!
ZIGGY
Tom Wilson

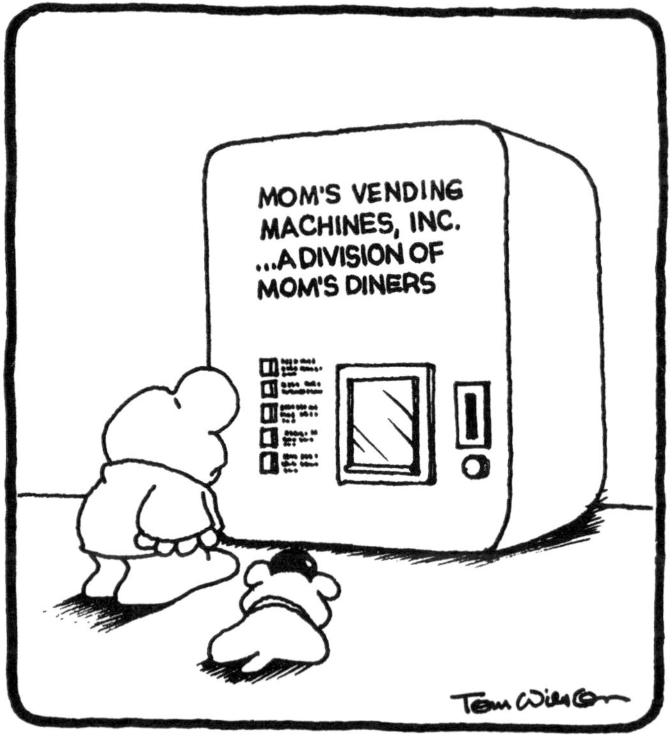
MOM'S VENDING MACHINES, INC. ...A DIVISION OF MOM'S DINERS
Tom Wilson

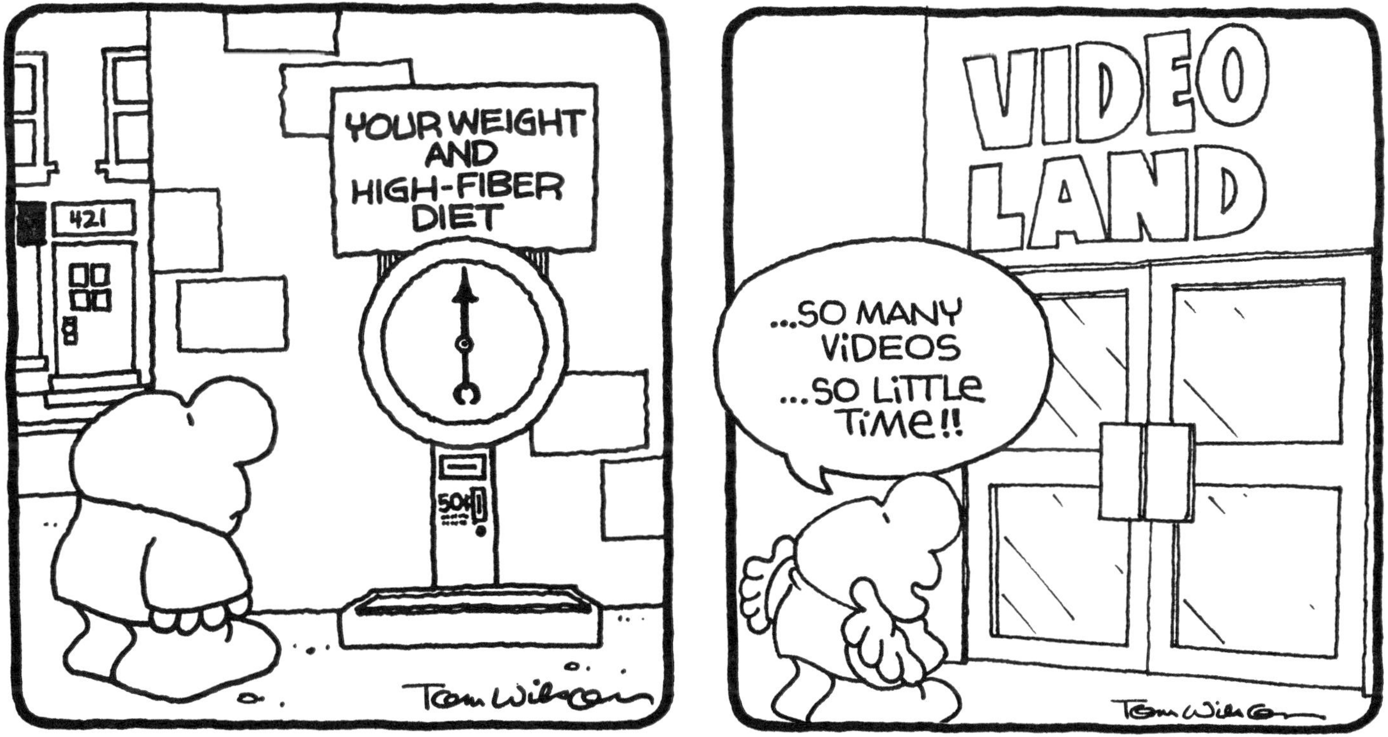
421
YOUR WEIGHT AND HIGH-FIBER DIET
50¢
Tom Wilson
VIDEO LAND
...SO MANY VIDEOS ...SO LITTLE TIME!!
Tom Wilson

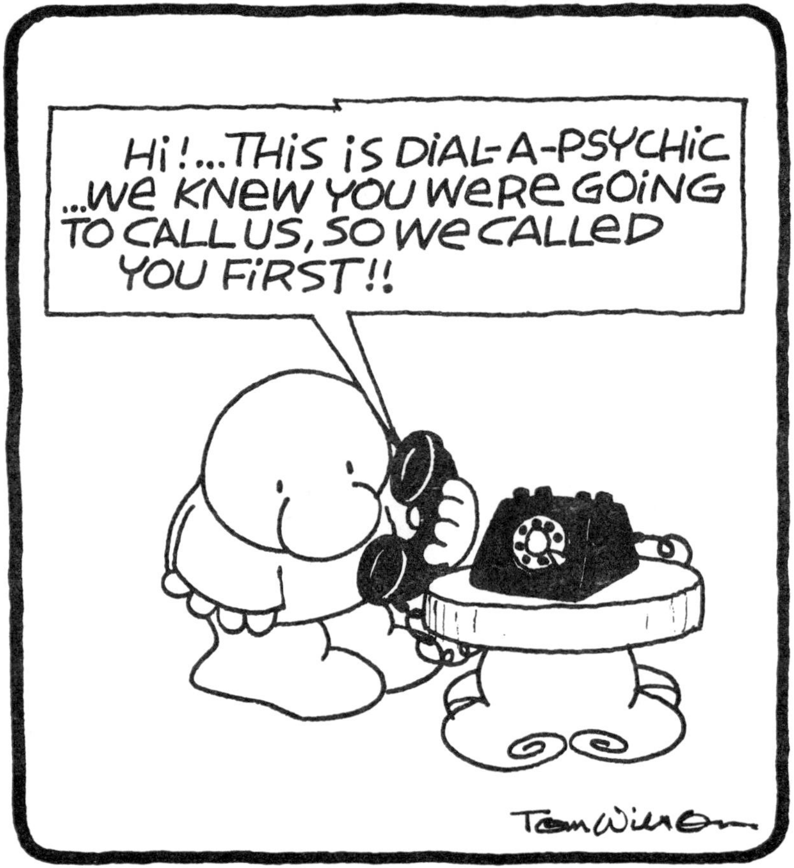
HI!...THIS IS DIAL-A-PSYCHIC ...WE KNEW YOU WERE GOING TO CALL US, SO WE CALLED YOU FIRST!!
Tom Wilson

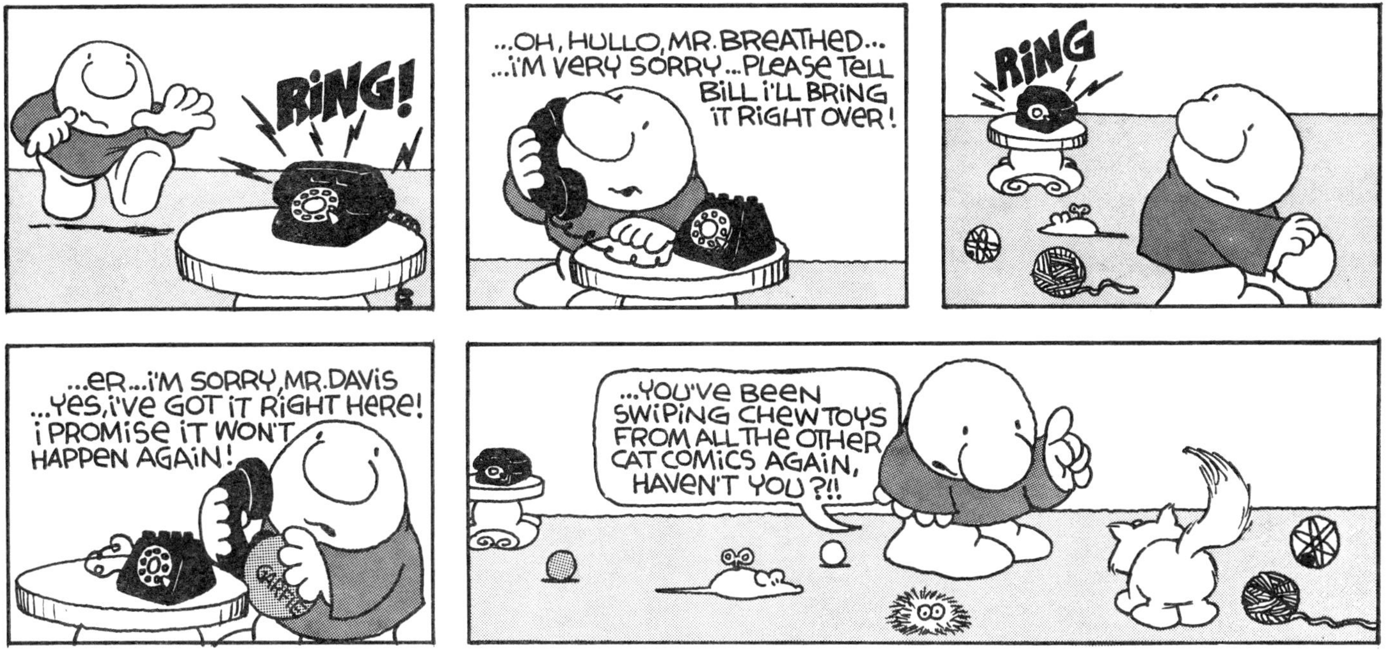
RING!
...OH, HULLO, MR. BREATHED... ...I'M VERY SORRY... PLEASE TELL BILL I'LL BRING IT RIGHT OVER!
RING
...ER...I'M SORRY, MR. DAVIS ...YES, I'VE GOT IT RIGHT HERE! I PROMISE IT WON'T HAPPEN AGAIN!
...YOU'VE BEEN SWIPING CHEW TOYS FROM ALL THE OTHER CAT COMICS AGAIN, HAVEN'T YOU?!!

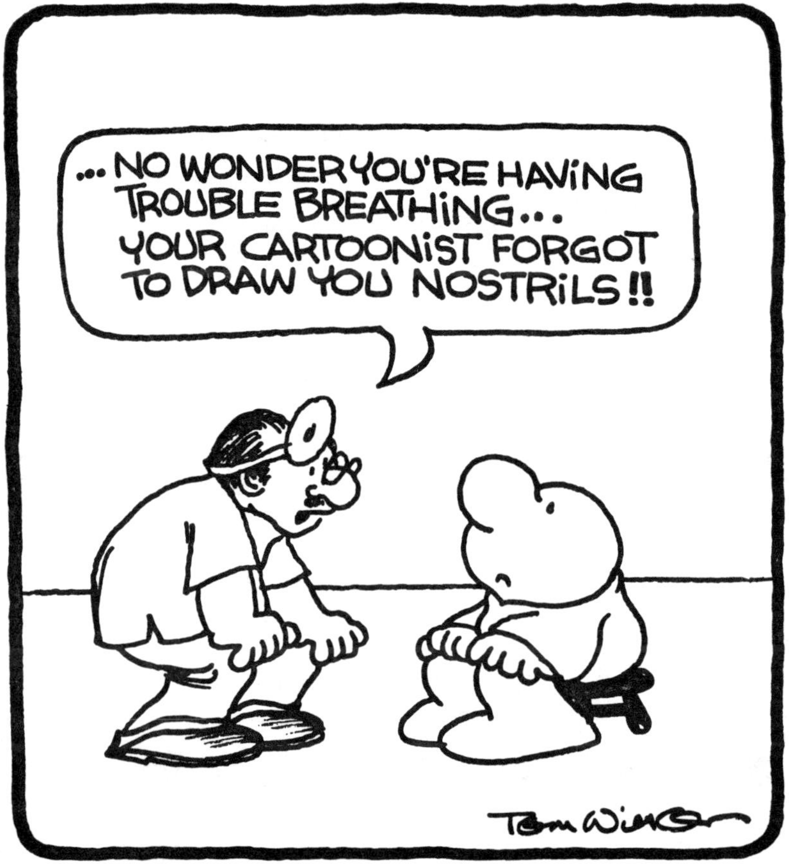
...NO WONDER YOU'RE HAVING TROUBLE BREATHING... YOUR CARTOONIST FORGOT TO DRAW YOU NOSTRILS!!
Tom Wilson

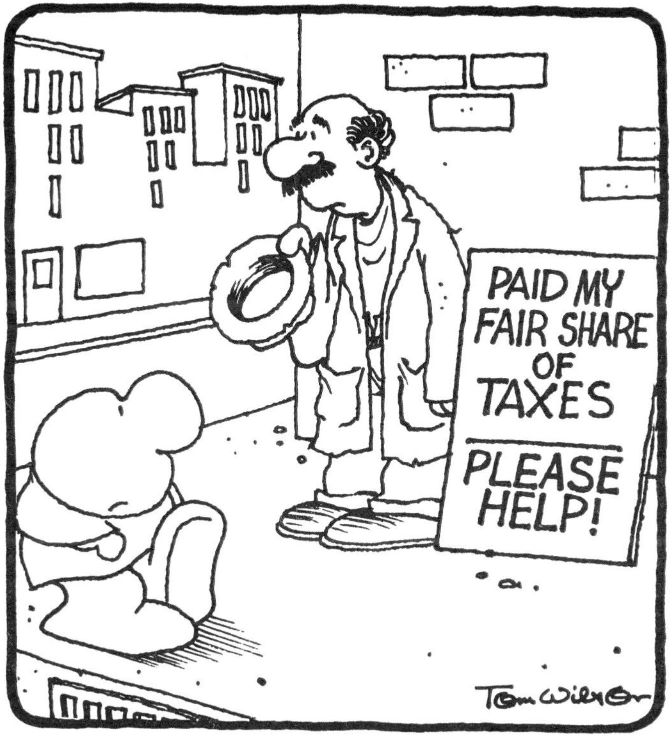
PAID MY FAIR SHARE OF TAXES
PLEASE HELP!
Tom Wilson

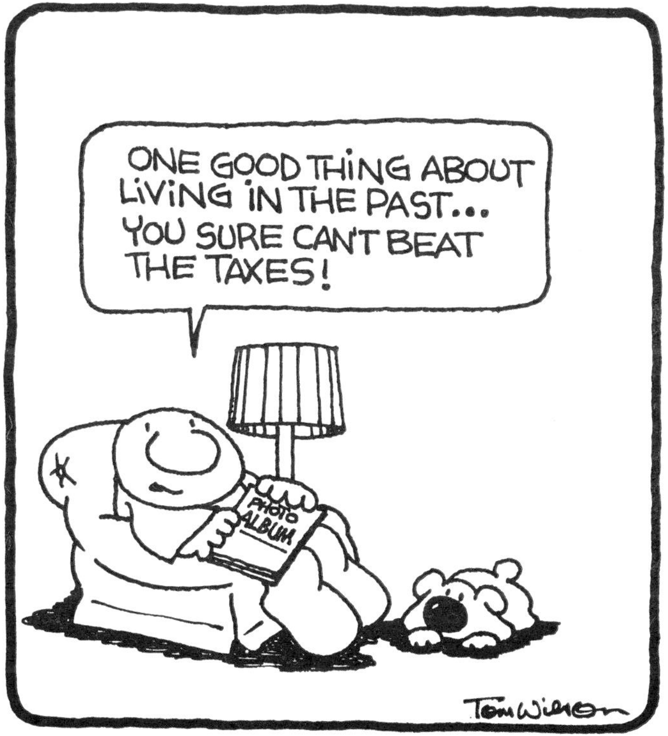
ONE GOOD THING ABOUT LIVING IN THE PAST... YOU SURE CAN'T BEAT THE TAXES!
PHOTO ALBUM
Tom Wilson

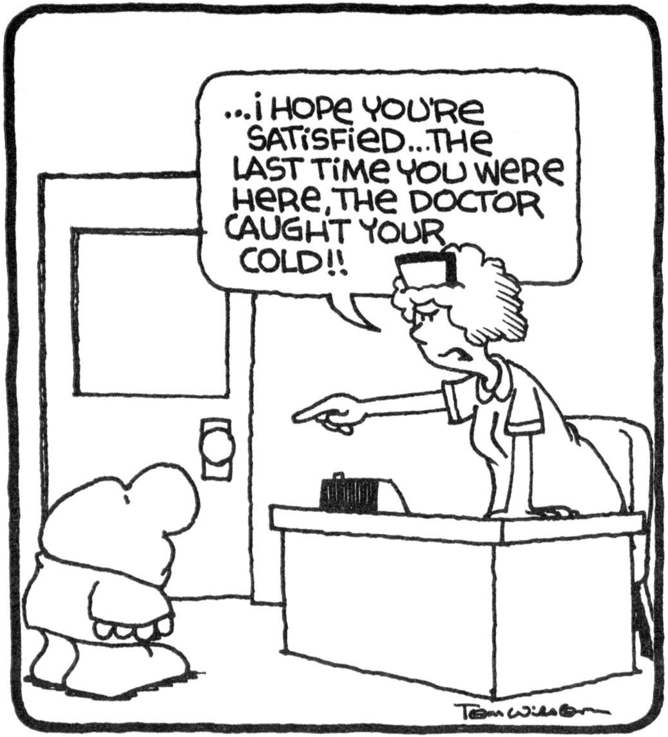
...i HOPE YOU'RE SATISFIED...THE LAST TIME YOU WERE HERE, THE DOCTOR CAUGHT YOUR COLD!!
Tom Wilson

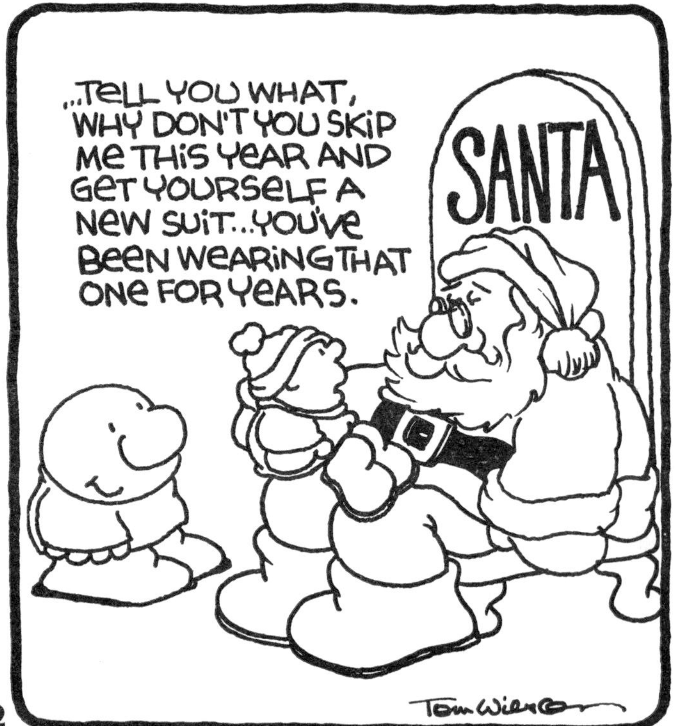
...TELL YOU WHAT, WHY DON'T YOU SKIP ME THIS YEAR AND GET YOURSELF A NEW SUIT...YOU'VE BEEN WEARING THAT ONE FOR YEARS.
SANTA
Tom Wilson

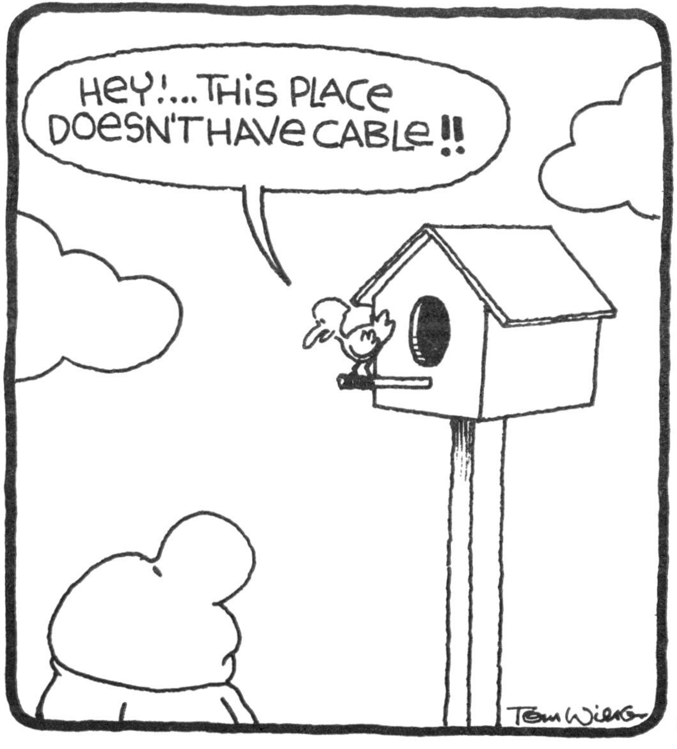
HEY!...THIS PLACE DOESN'T HAVE CABLE!!
TOM WILSON

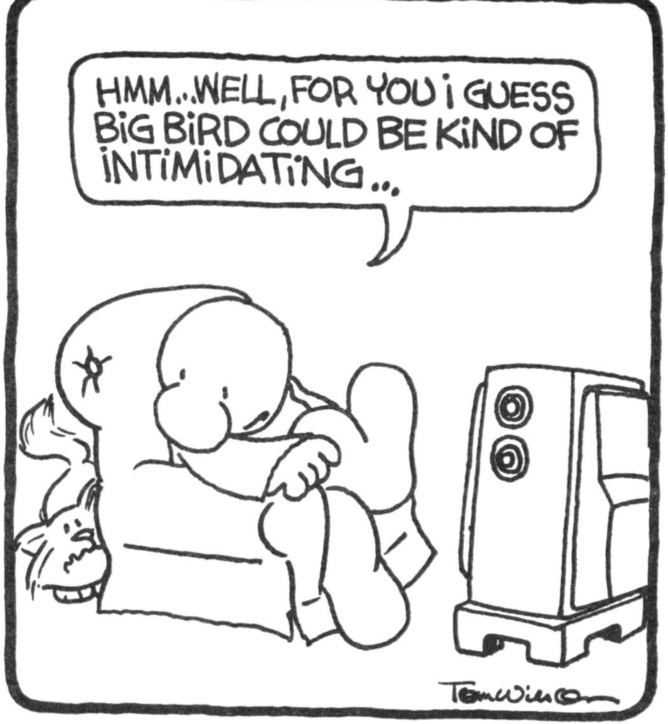
HMM...WELL, FOR YOU I GUESS BIG BIRD COULD BE KIND OF INTIMIDATING...
TOM WILSON

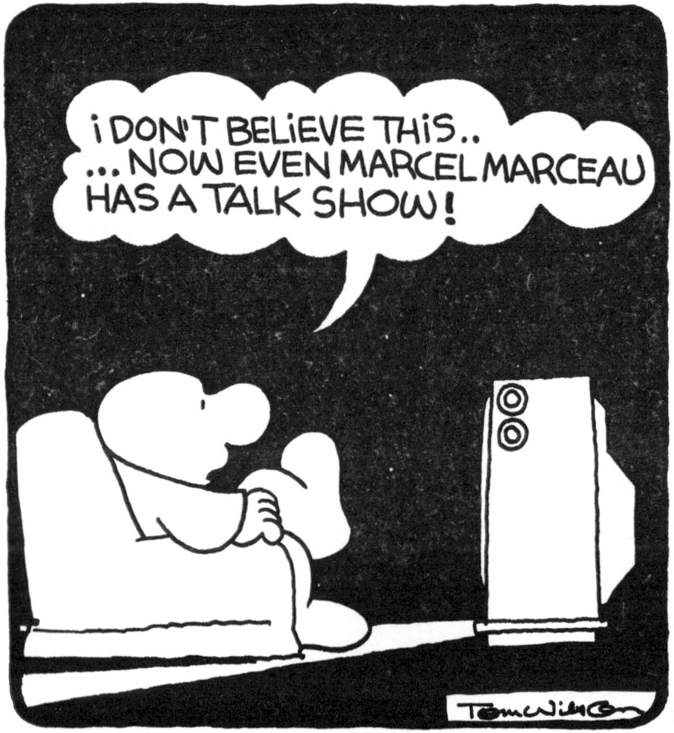
I DON'T BELIEVE THIS..
... NOW EVEN MARCEL MARCEAU HAS A TALK SHOW!
Tom Wilson

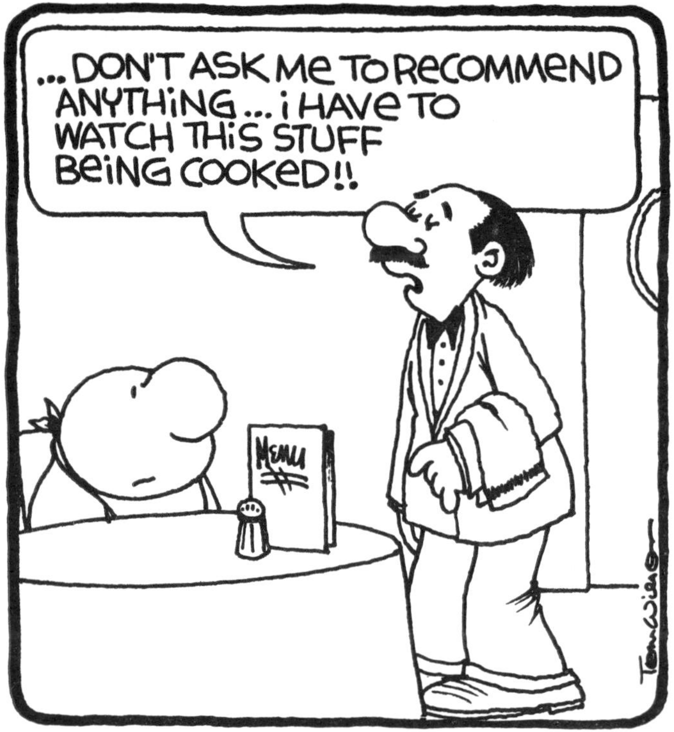
... DON'T ASK ME TO RECOMMEND ANYTHING ... I HAVE TO WATCH THIS STUFF BEING COOKED!!
MENU
Tom Wilson

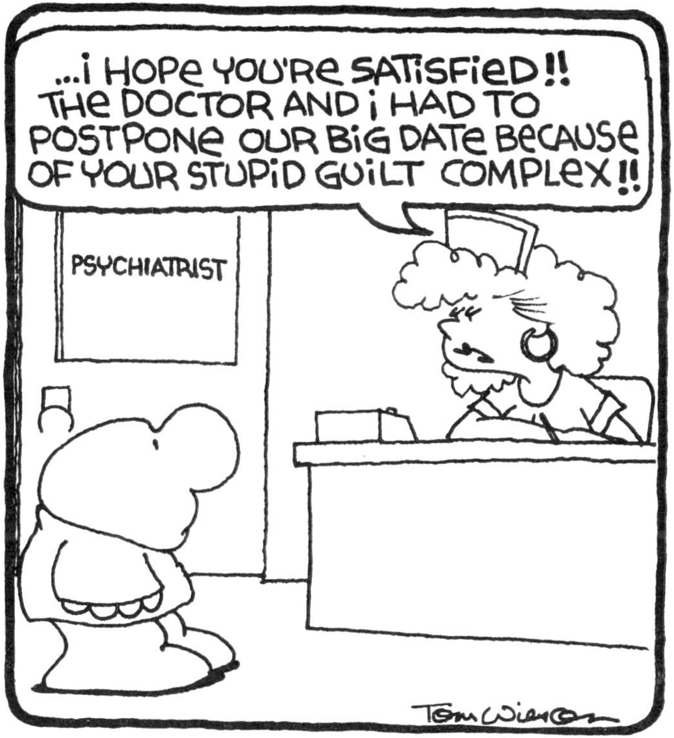
...i HOPE YOU'RE SATISFIED!! THE DOCTOR AND i HAD TO POSTPONE OUR BIG DATE BECAUSE OF YOUR STUPID GUILT COMPLEX!!
PSYCHIATRIST
TOM WILSON

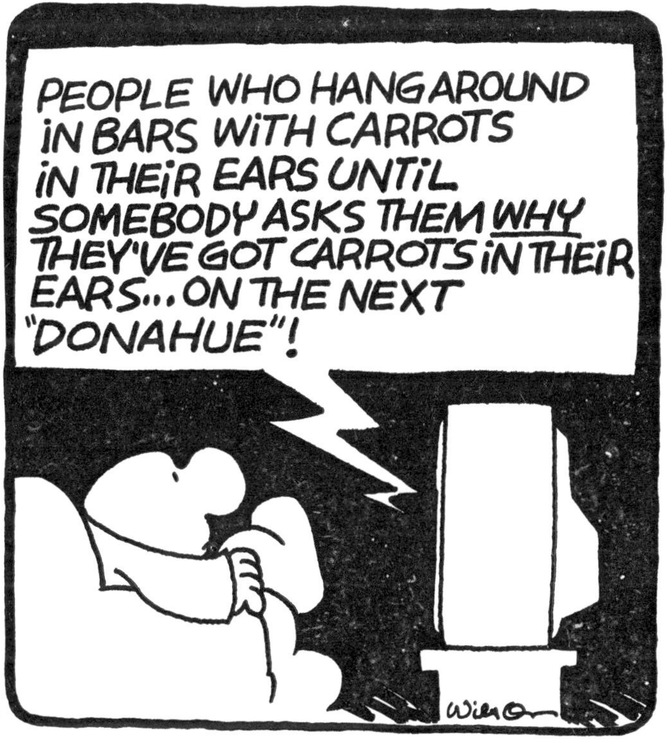
PEOPLE WHO HANG AROUND iN BARS WiTH CARROTS iN THEiR EARS UNTiL SOMEBODY ASKS THEM WHY THEY'VE GOT CARROTS iN THEiR EARS...ON THE NEXT "DONAHUE"!
WILSON

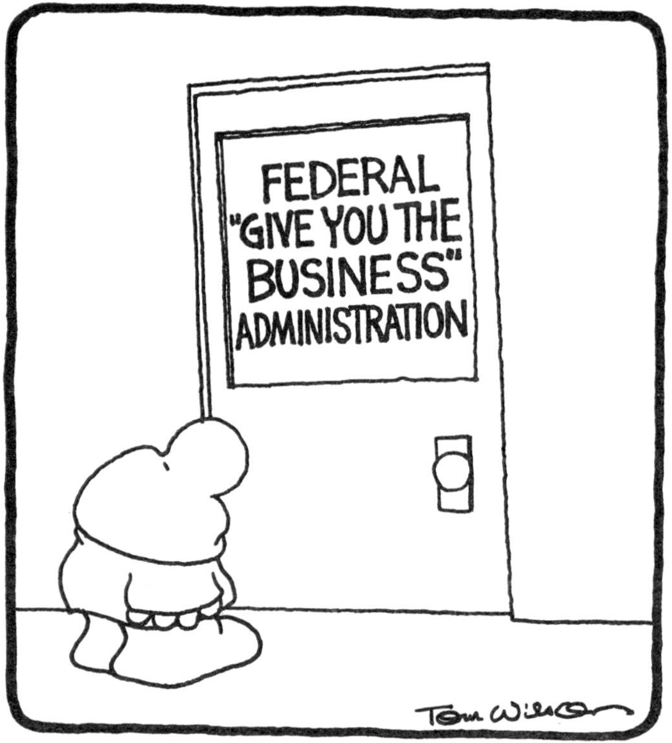
FEDERAL "GIVE YOU THE BUSINESS" ADMINISTRATION
Tom Wilson

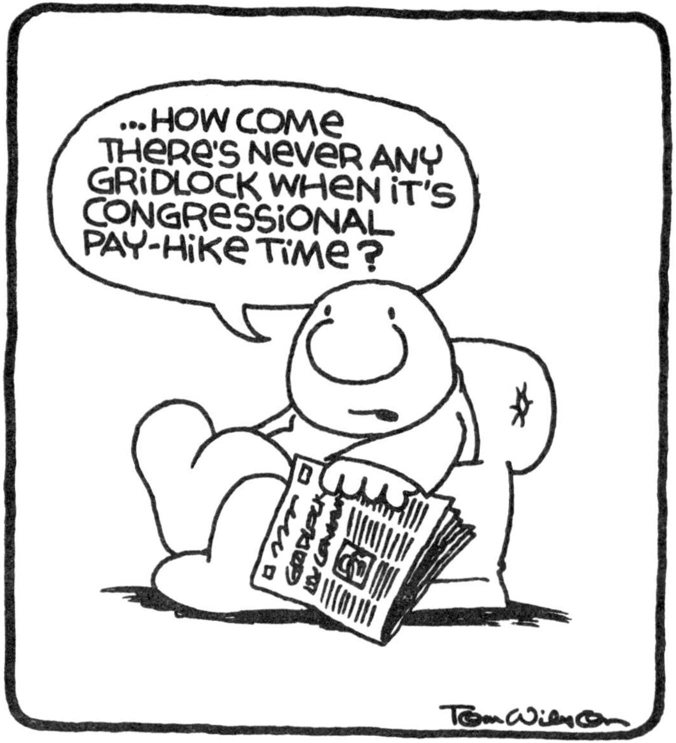
...HOW COME THERE'S NEVER ANY GRIDLOCK WHEN IT'S CONGRESSIONAL PAY-HIKE TIME?
Tom Wilson

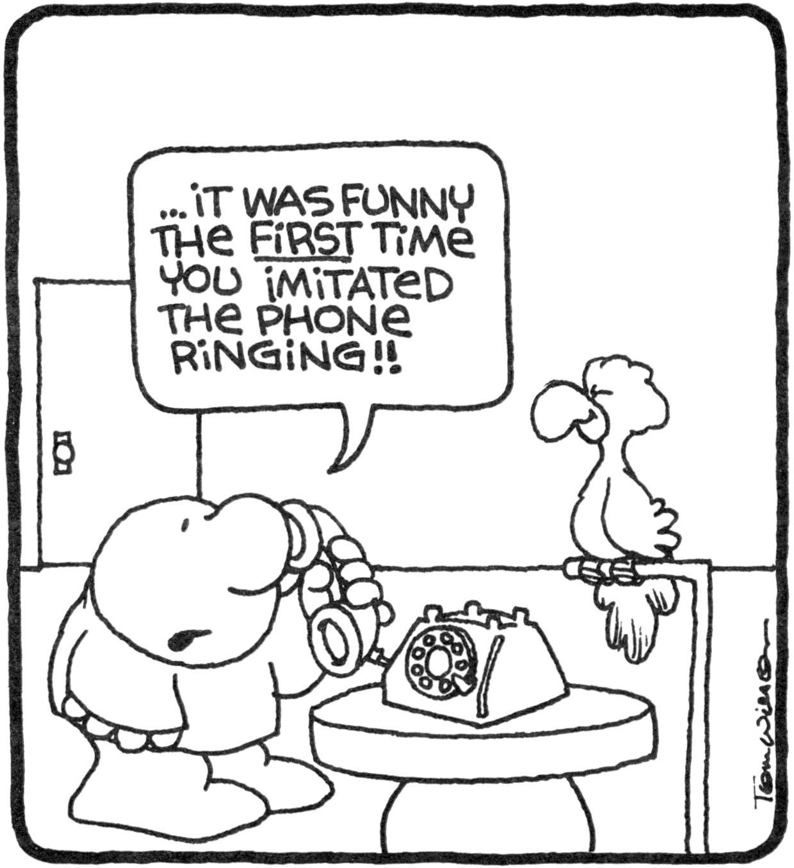
...IT WAS FUNNY THE FIRST TIME YOU IMITATED THE PHONE RINGING!!
Tom Wilson

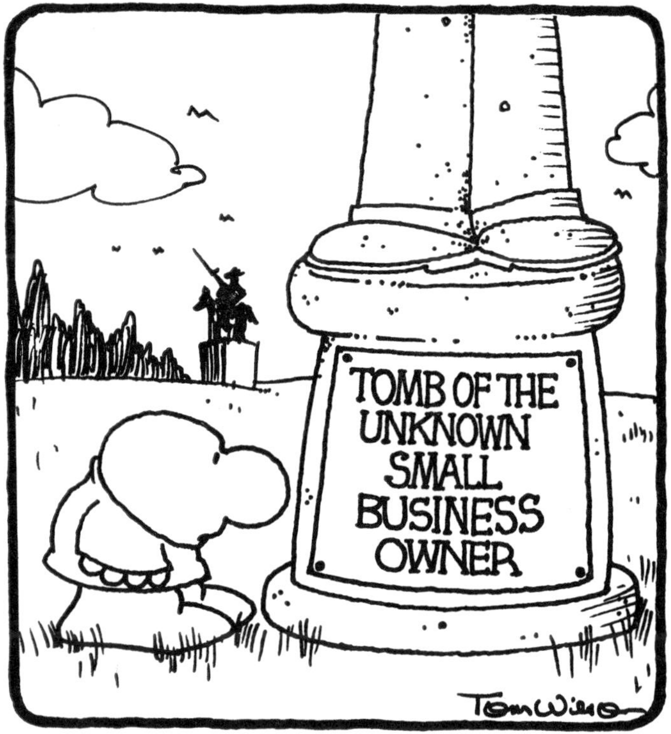
TOMB OF THE UNKNOWN SMALL BUSINESS OWNER
Tom Wilson

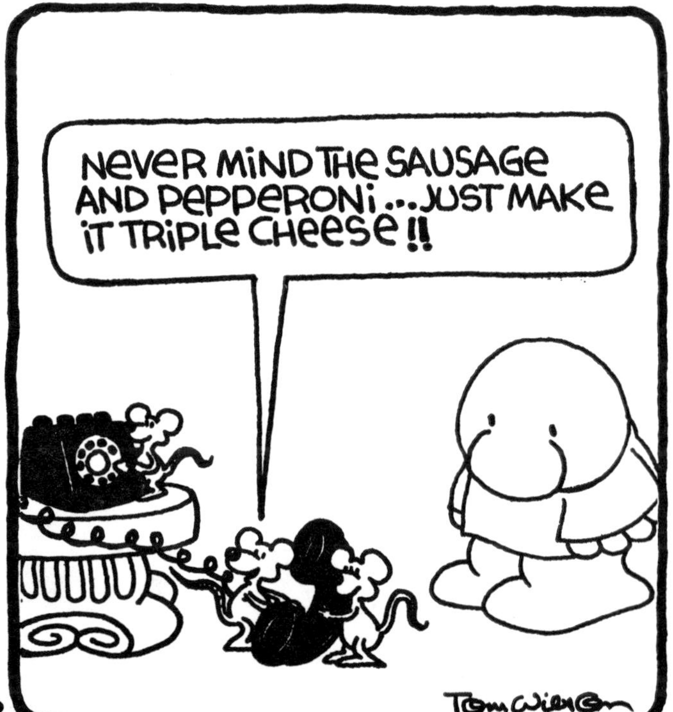
NEVER MIND THE SAUSAGE AND PEPPERONI ... JUST MAKE IT TRIPLE CHEESE !!
Tom Wilson

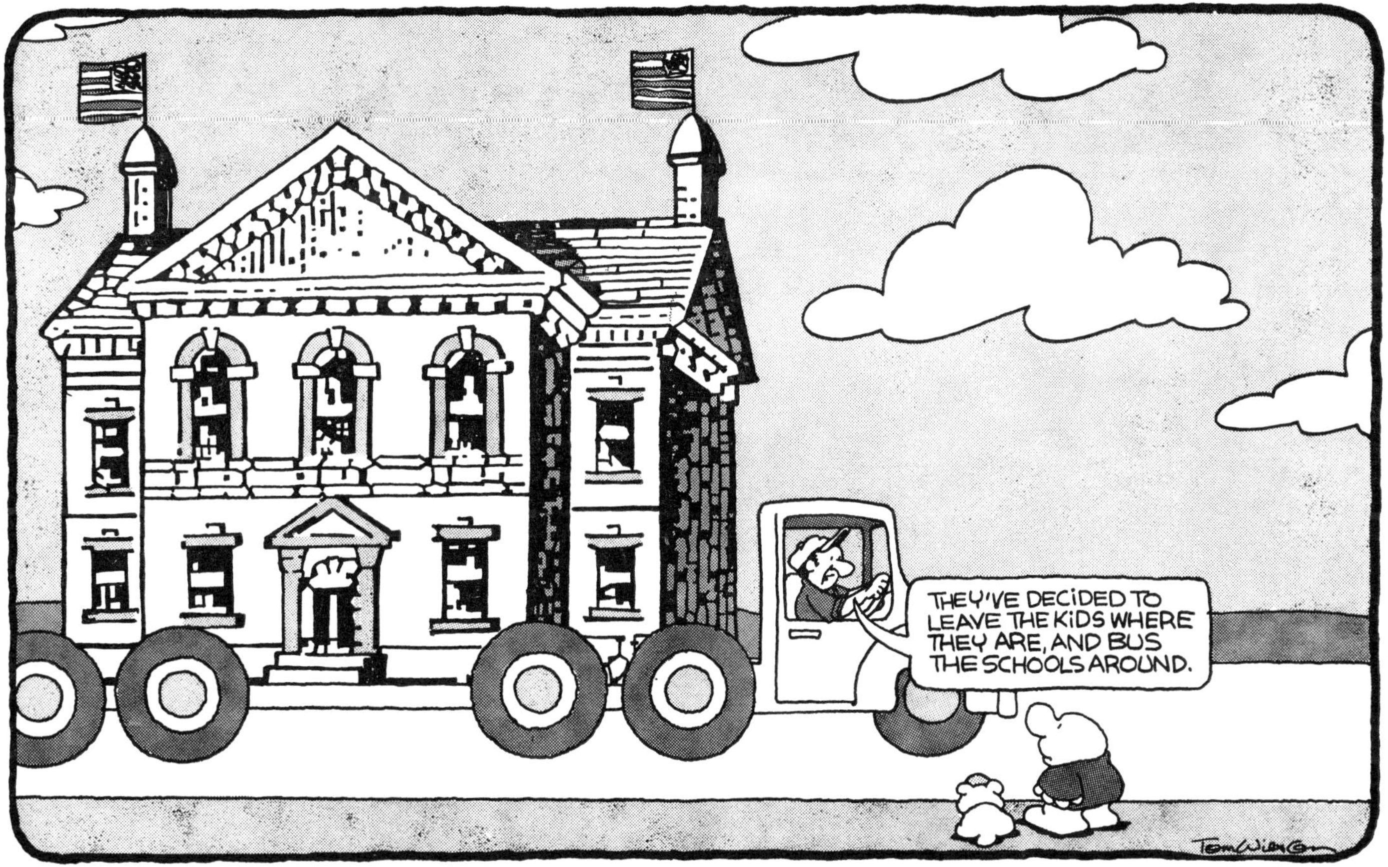
THEY'VE DECIDED TO LEAVE THE KIDS WHERE THEY ARE, AND BUS THE SCHOOLS AROUND.
TOM WILSON

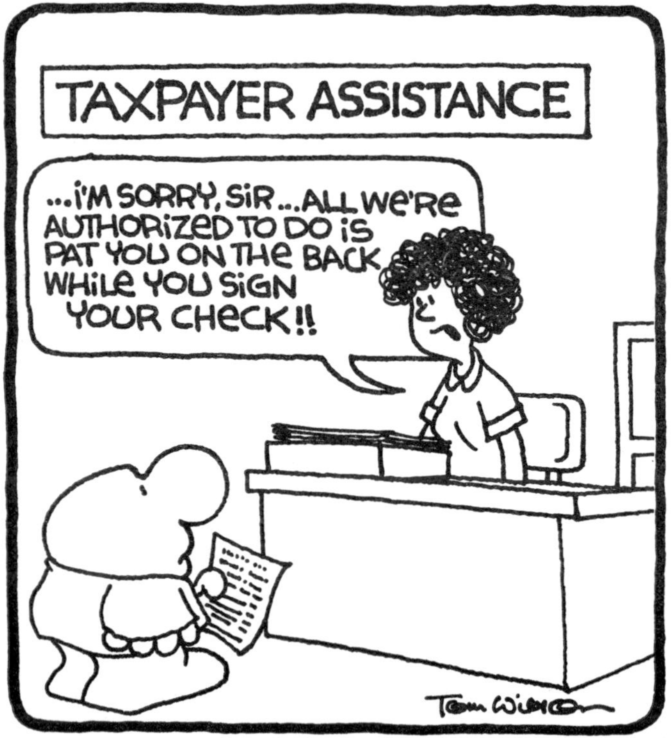
TAXPAYER ASSISTANCE
...I'M SORRY, SIR...ALL WE'RE AUTHORIZED TO DO IS PAT YOU ON THE BACK WHILE YOU SIGN YOUR CHECK!!
Tom Wilson

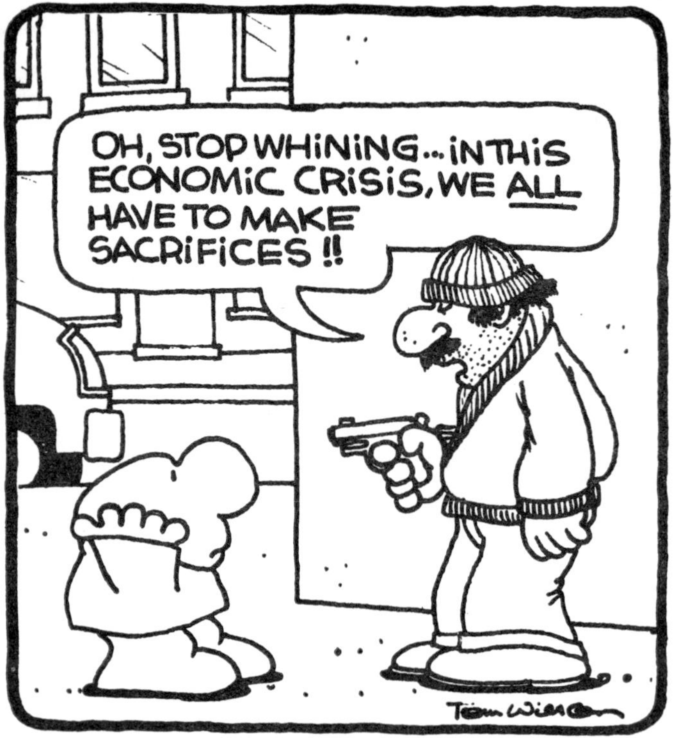
OH, STOP WHINING...IN THIS ECONOMIC CRISIS, WE ALL HAVE TO MAKE SACRIFICES!!
Tom Wilson

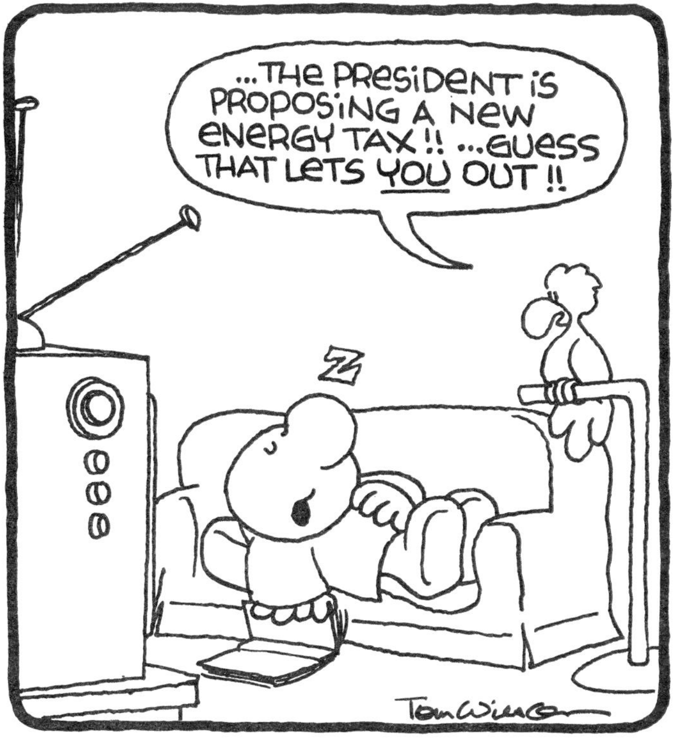
...THE PRESIDENT IS PROPOSING A NEW ENERGY TAX !! ...GUESS THAT LETS YOU OUT !!
TOM WILSON

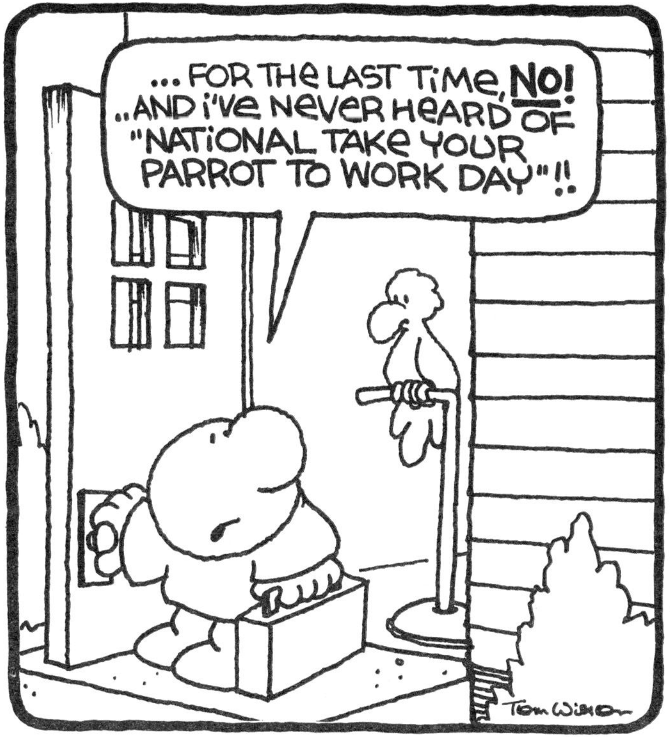
... FOR THE LAST TIME, NO! ..AND I'VE NEVER HEARD OF "NATIONAL TAKE YOUR PARROT TO WORK DAY"!!
TOM WILSON

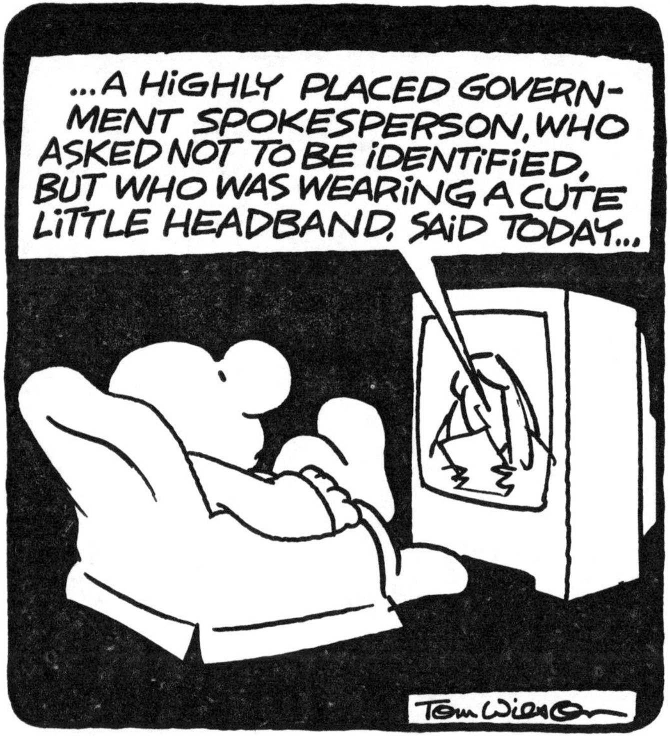
...A HIGHLY PLACED GOVERNMENT SPOKESPERSON, WHO ASKED NOT TO BE IDENTIFIED, BUT WHO WAS WEARING A CUTE LITTLE HEADBAND, SAID TODAY...
TOM WILSON

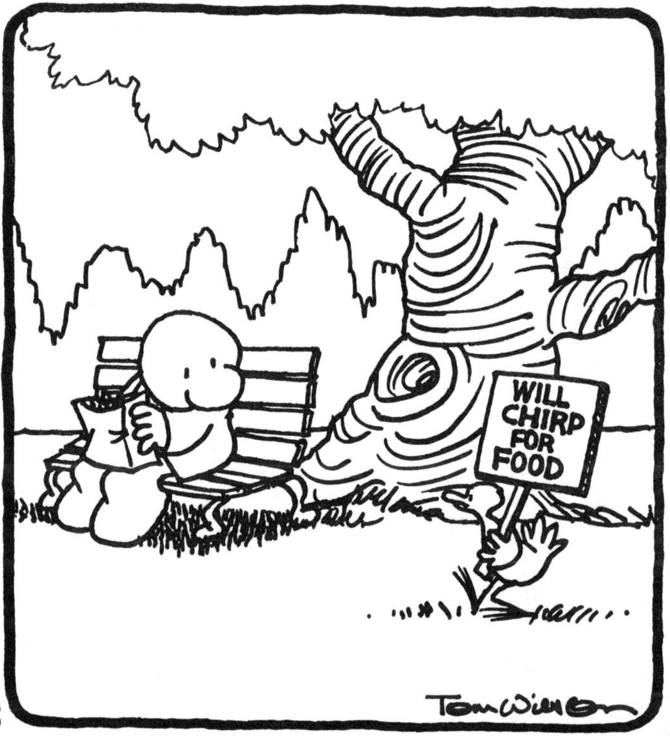
WILL CHIRP FOR FOOD
TOM WILSON

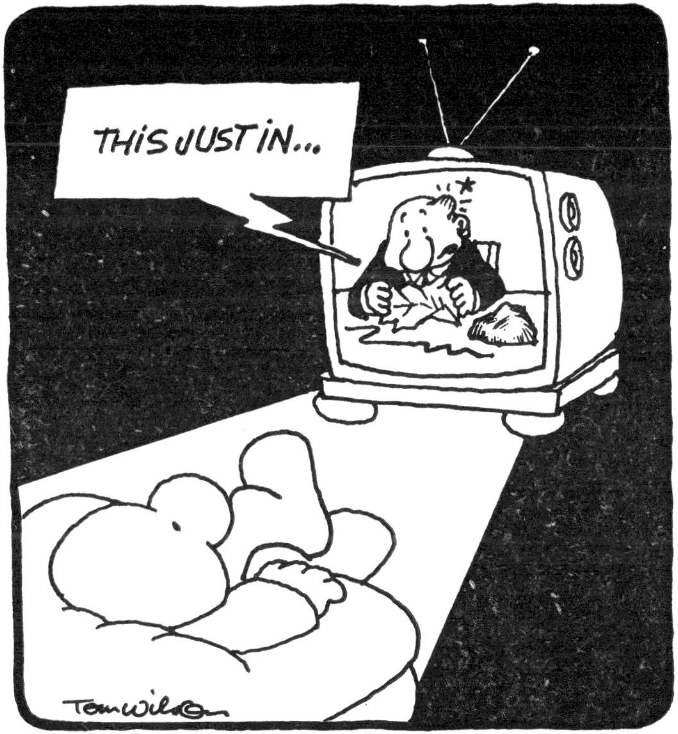
THIS JUST IN...

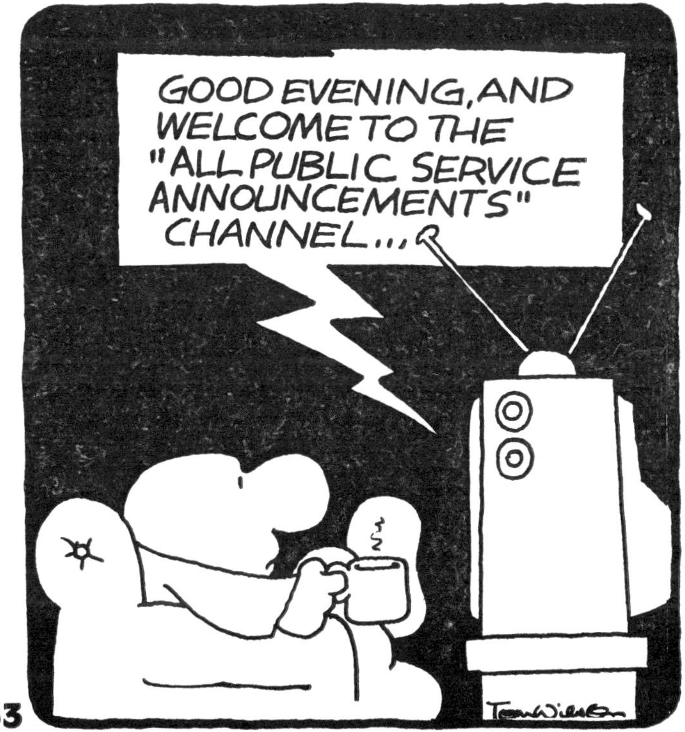
GOOD EVENING, AND WELCOME TO THE "ALL PUBLIC SERVICE ANNOUNCEMENTS" CHANNEL...

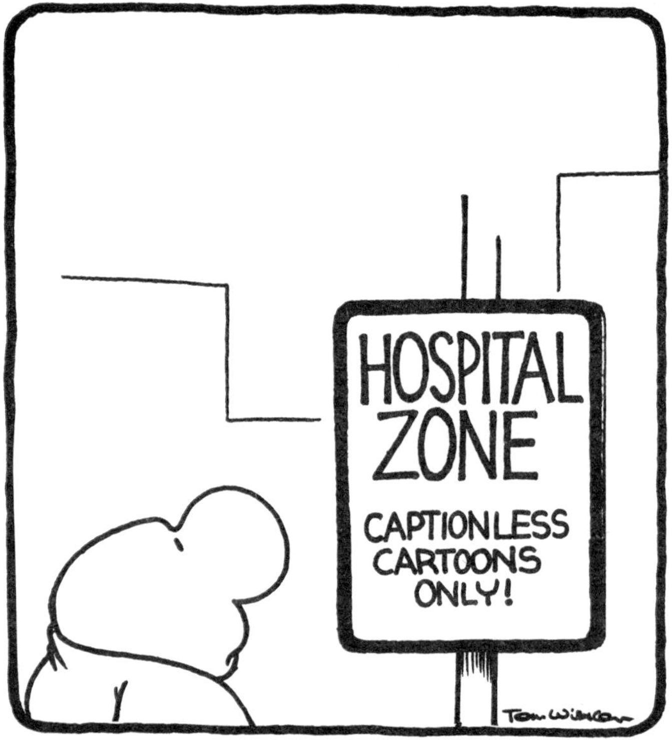
HOSPITAL ZONE
CAPTIONLESS CARTOONS ONLY!
Tom Wilson

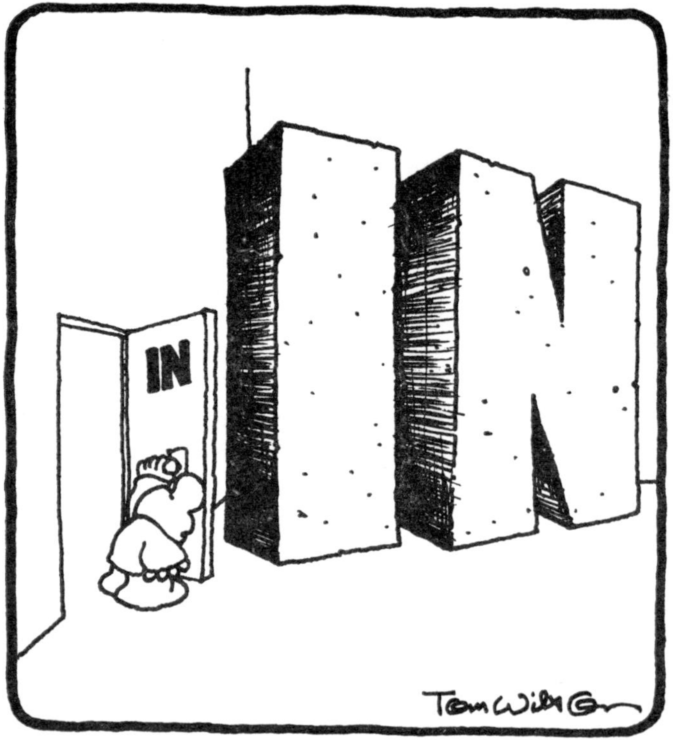
IN
Tom Wilson

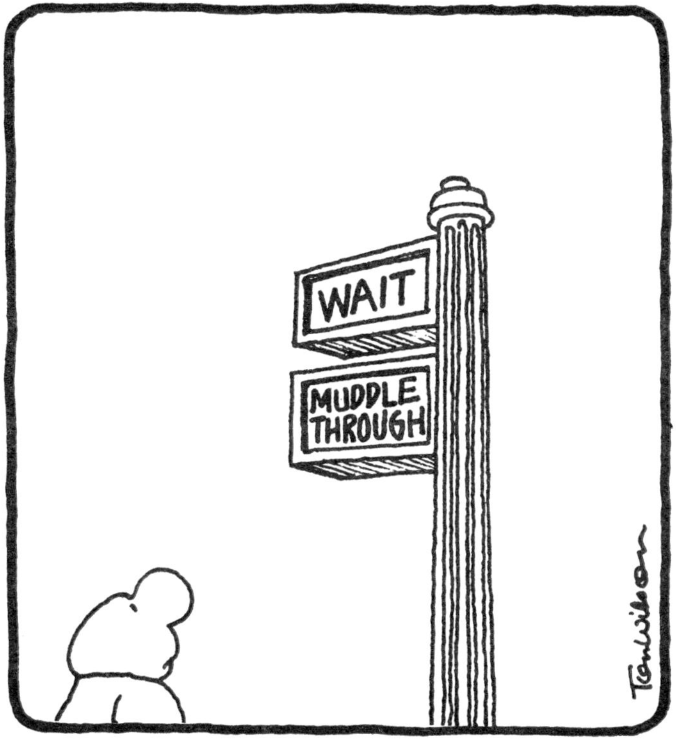
WAIT
MUDDLE THROUGH
Tom Wilson

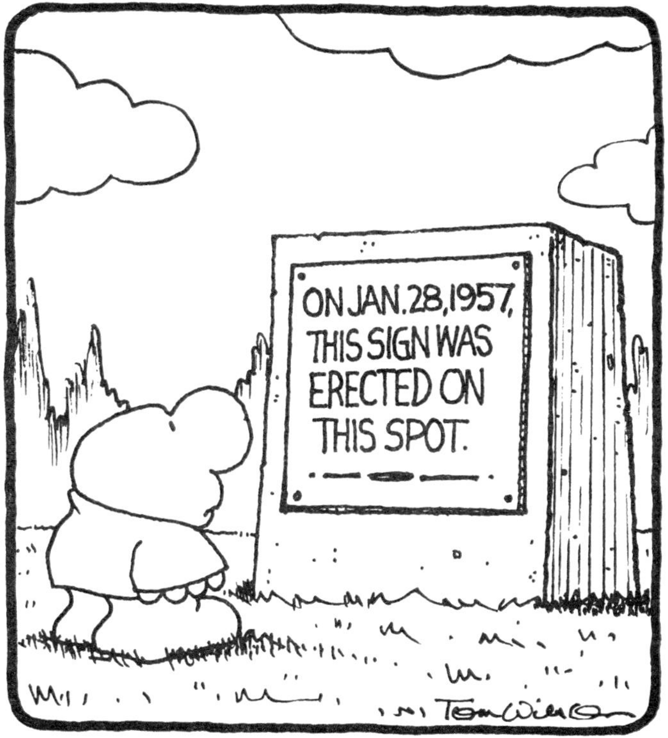
ON JAN. 28, 1957, THIS SIGN WAS ERECTED ON THIS SPOT.
Tom Wilson

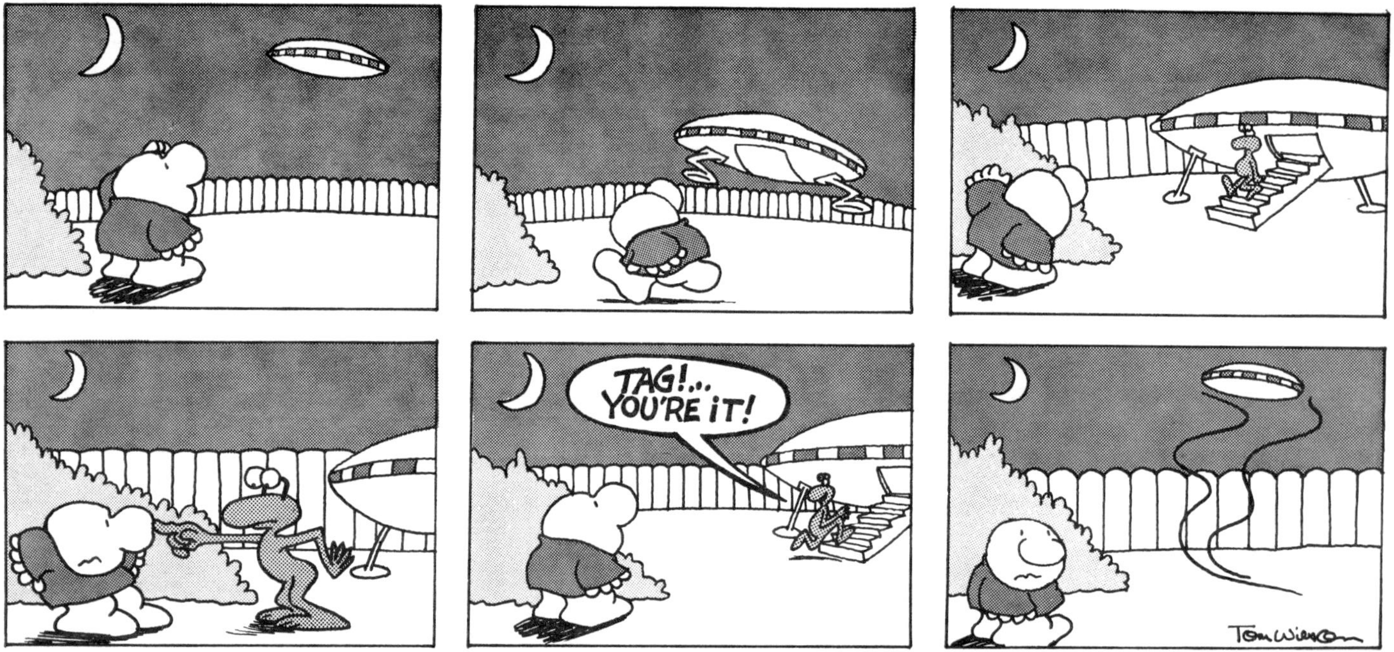
TAG!... YOU'RE IT!
TOM WILSON

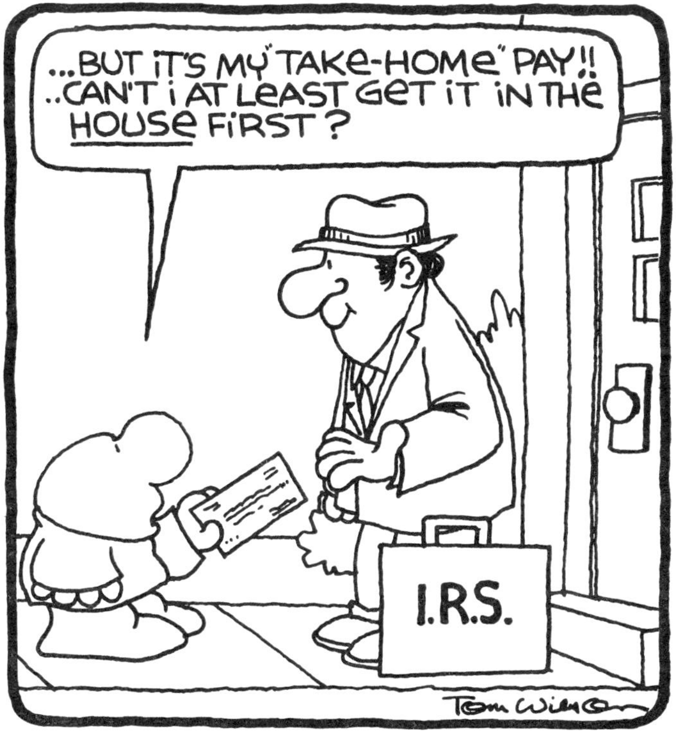
...BUT IT'S MY "TAKE-HOME" PAY!! ..CAN'T I AT LEAST GET IT IN THE HOUSE FIRST?
I.R.S.
TOM WILSON

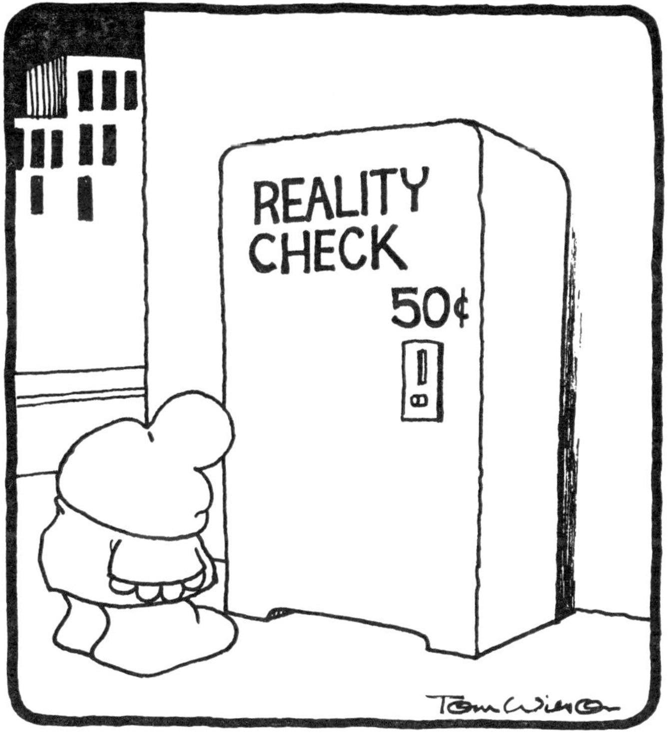
REALITY CHECK
50¢
TOM WILSON

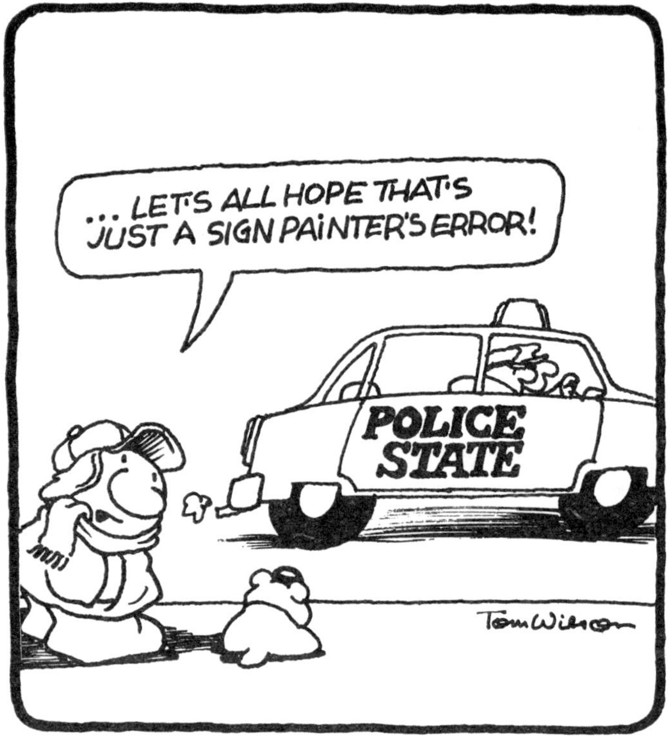
... LET'S ALL HOPE THAT'S JUST A SIGN PAINTER'S ERROR!
POLICE STATE
Tom Wilson

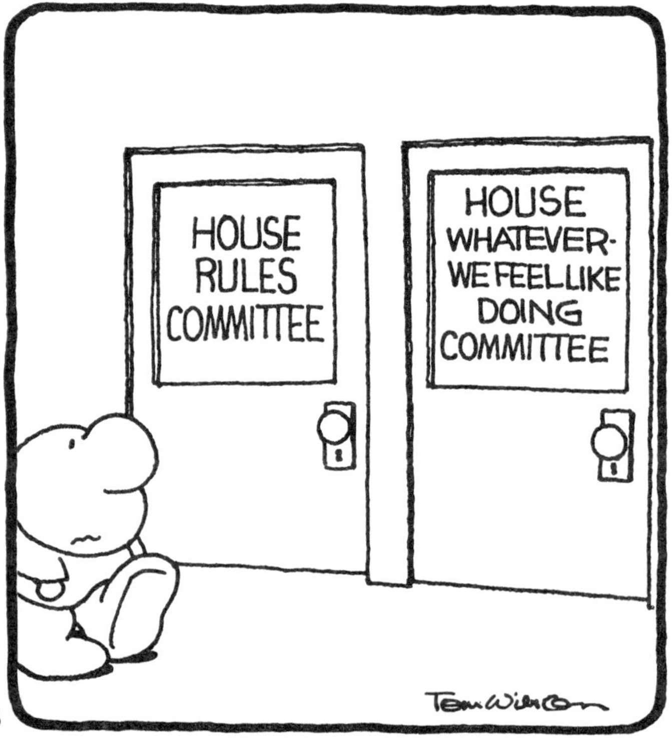
HOUSE RULES COMMITTEE
HOUSE WHATEVER-WE FEEL LIKE DOING COMMITTEE
Tom Wilson

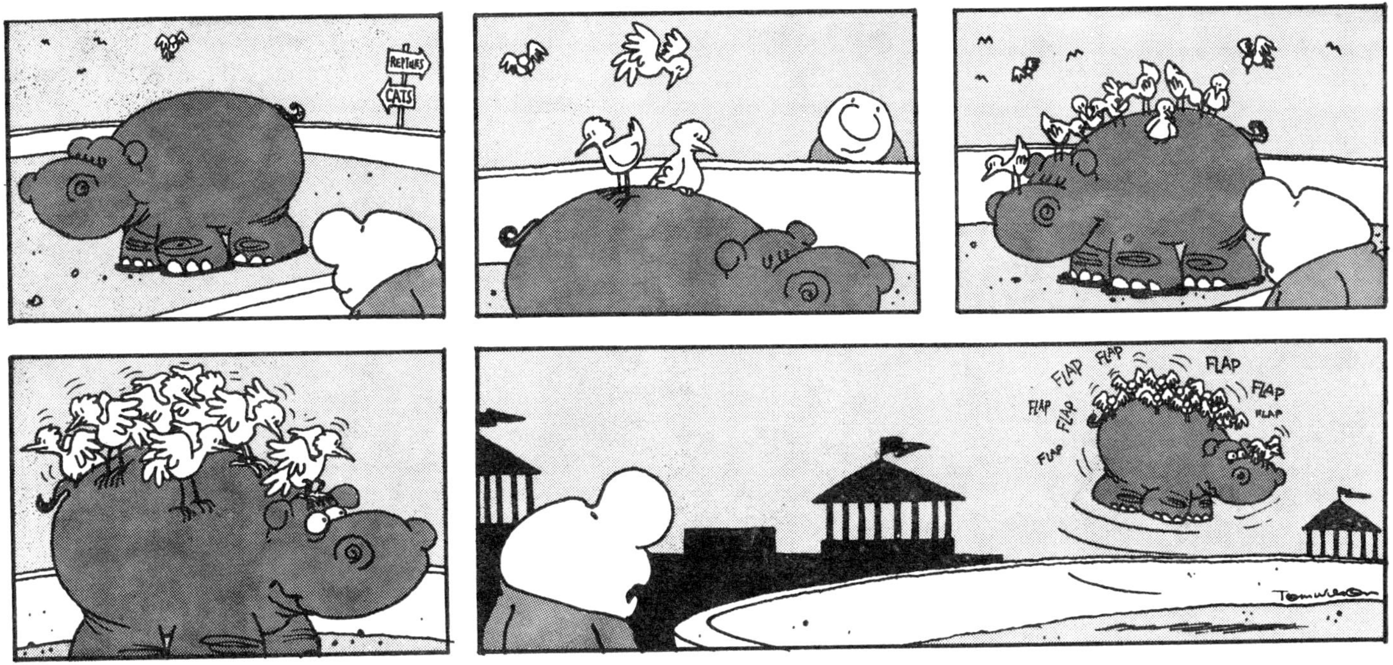
REPTILES
CATS
FLAP
FLAP
FLAP
FLAP
FLAP
FLAP
FLAP
FLAP

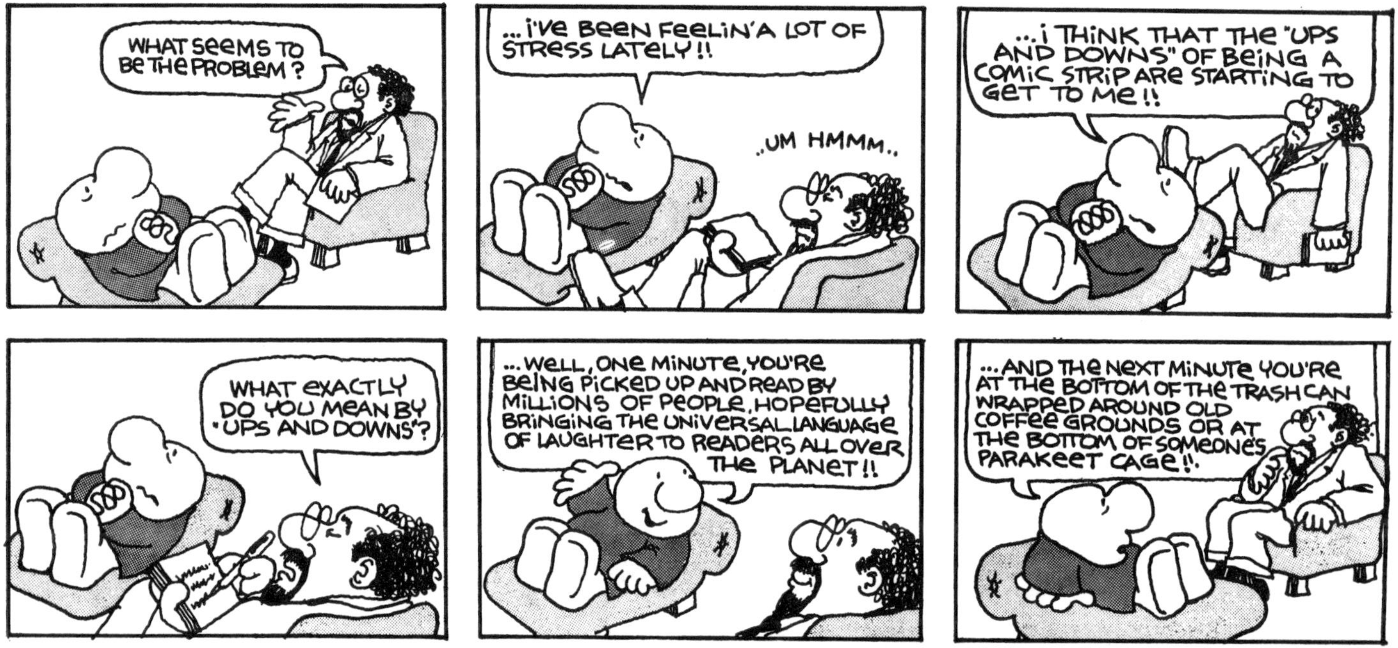
WHAT SEEMS TO BE THE PROBLEM?
...I'VE BEEN FEELIN' A LOT OF STRESS LATELY!!
..UM HMMM..
...I THINK THAT THE "UPS AND DOWNS" OF BEING A COMIC STRIP ARE STARTING TO GET TO ME!!
WHAT EXACTLY DO YOU MEAN BY "UPS AND DOWNS"?
...WELL, ONE MINUTE, YOU'RE BEING PICKED UP AND READ BY MILLIONS OF PEOPLE, HOPEFULLY BRINGING THE UNIVERSAL LANGUAGE OF LAUGHTER TO READERS ALL OVER THE PLANET!!
...AND THE NEXT MINUTE YOU'RE AT THE BOTTOM OF THE TRASH CAN WRAPPED AROUND OLD COFFEE GROUNDS OR AT THE BOTTOM OF SOMEONE'S PARAKEET CAGE!!

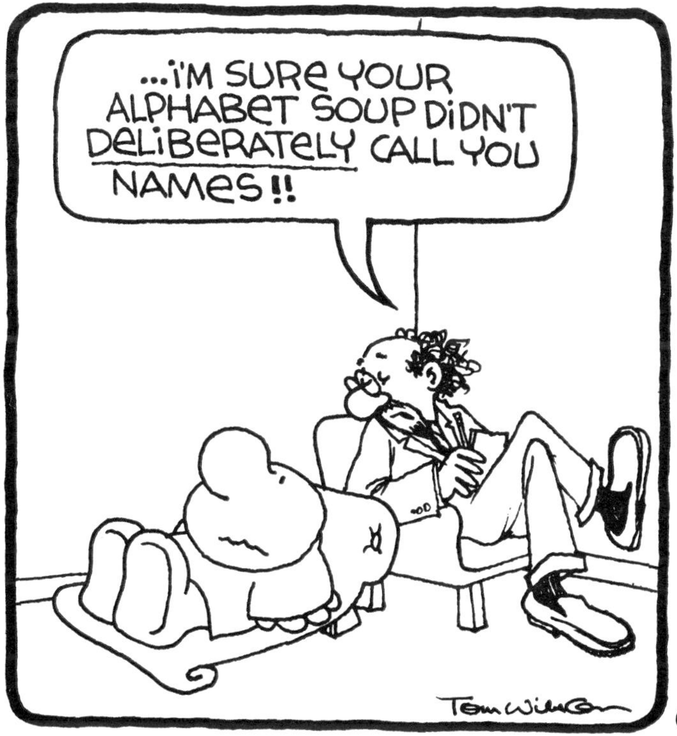
...I'M SURE YOUR ALPHABET SOUP DIDN'T DELIBERATELY CALL YOU NAMES!!
Tom Wilson

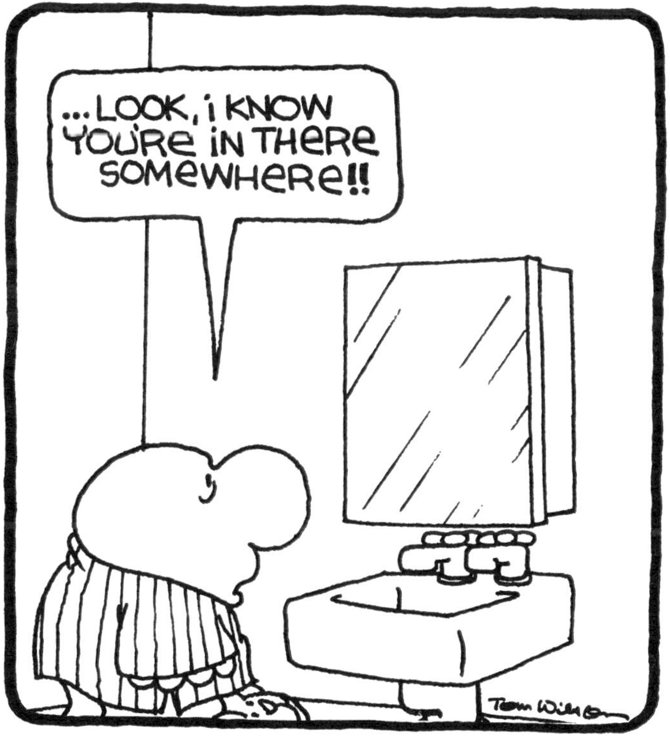
...LOOK, I KNOW YOU'RE IN THERE SOMEWHERE!!
Tom Wilson

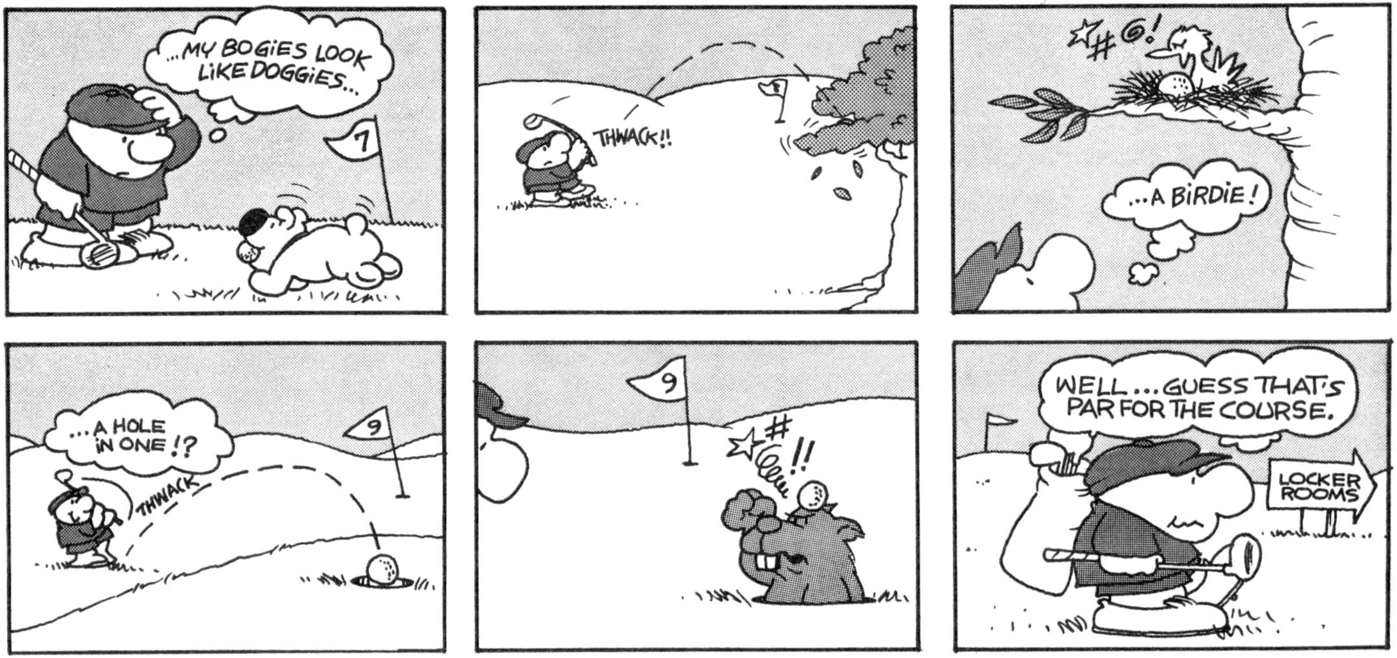
...MY BOGIES LOOK LIKE DOGGIES...
7
THWACK!!
...A BIRDIE!
...A HOLE IN ONE!?
9
THWACK
9
WELL...GUESS THAT'S PAR FOR THE COURSE.
LOCKER ROOMS

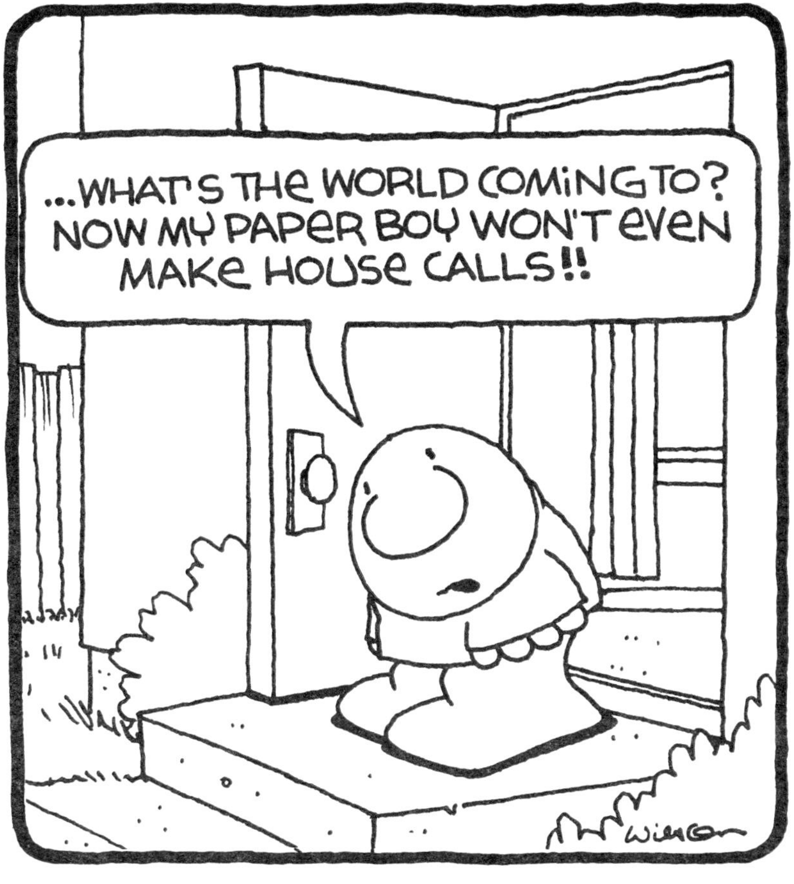
...WHAT'S THE WORLD COMING TO? NOW MY PAPER BOY WON'T EVEN MAKE HOUSE CALLS!!
WILSON

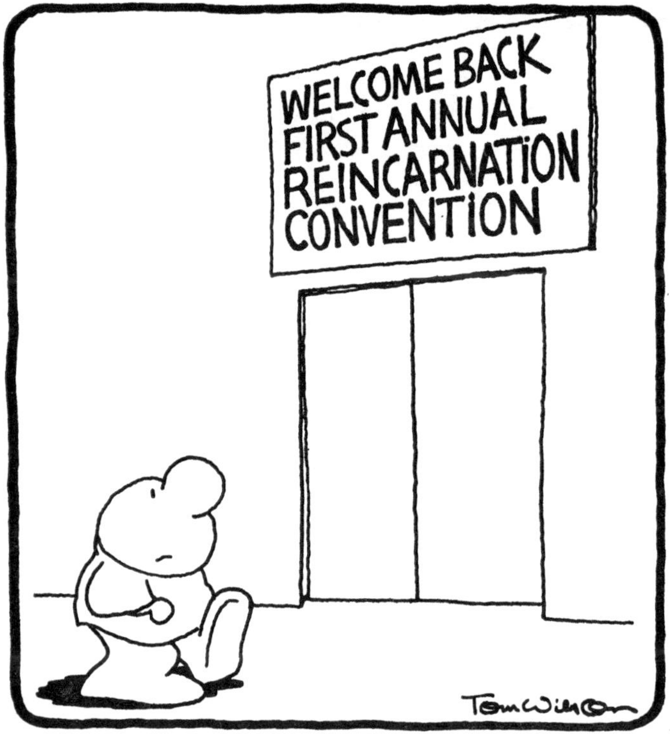
WELCOME BACK
FIRST ANNUAL
REINCARNATION
CONVENTION
Tom Wilson

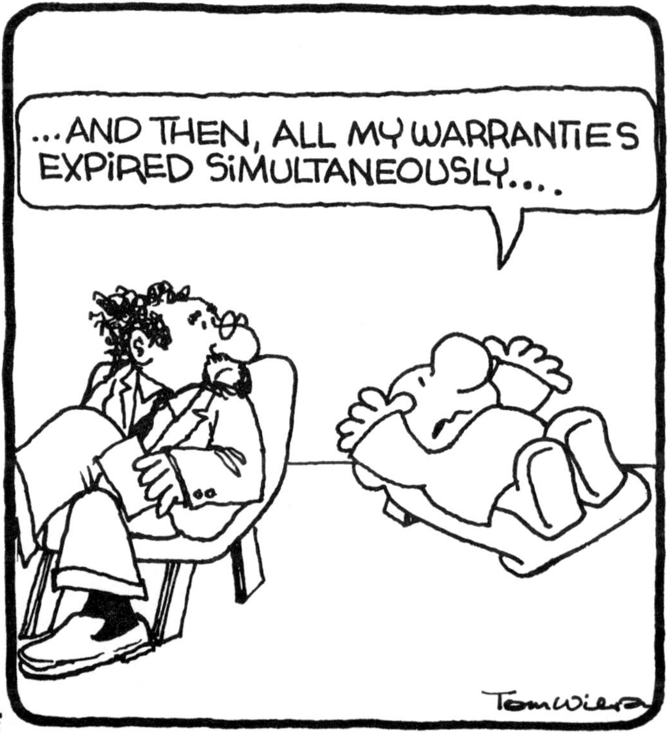
...AND THEN, ALL MY WARRANTIES EXPIRED SIMULTANEOUSLY....
Tom Wilson

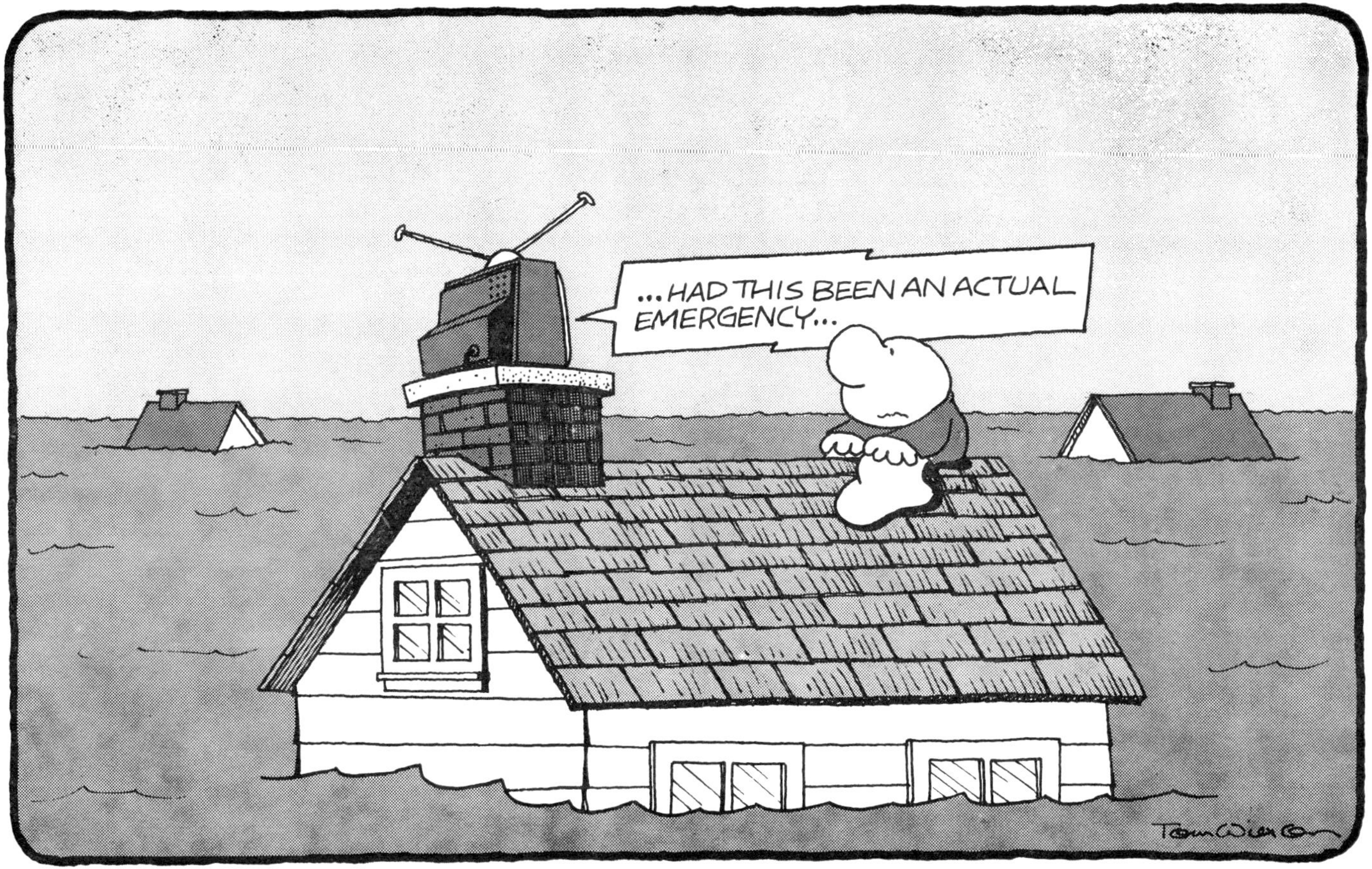
...HAD THIS BEEN AN ACTUAL EMERGENCY...
Tom Wilson

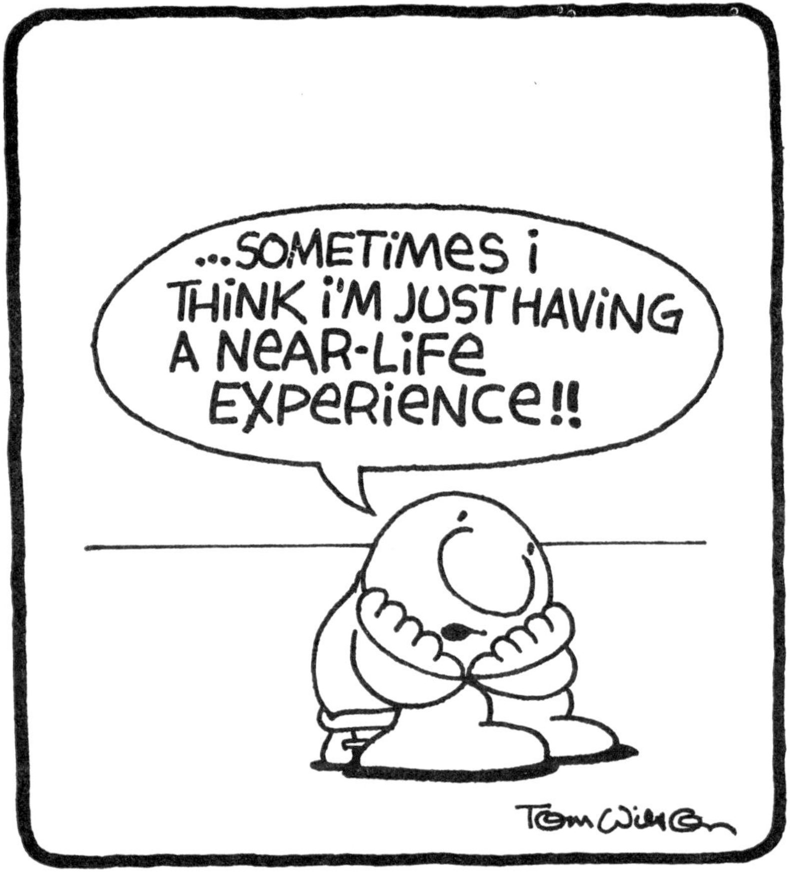
...SOMETIMES I THINK I'M JUST HAVING A NEAR-LIFE EXPERIENCE!!
Tom Wilson

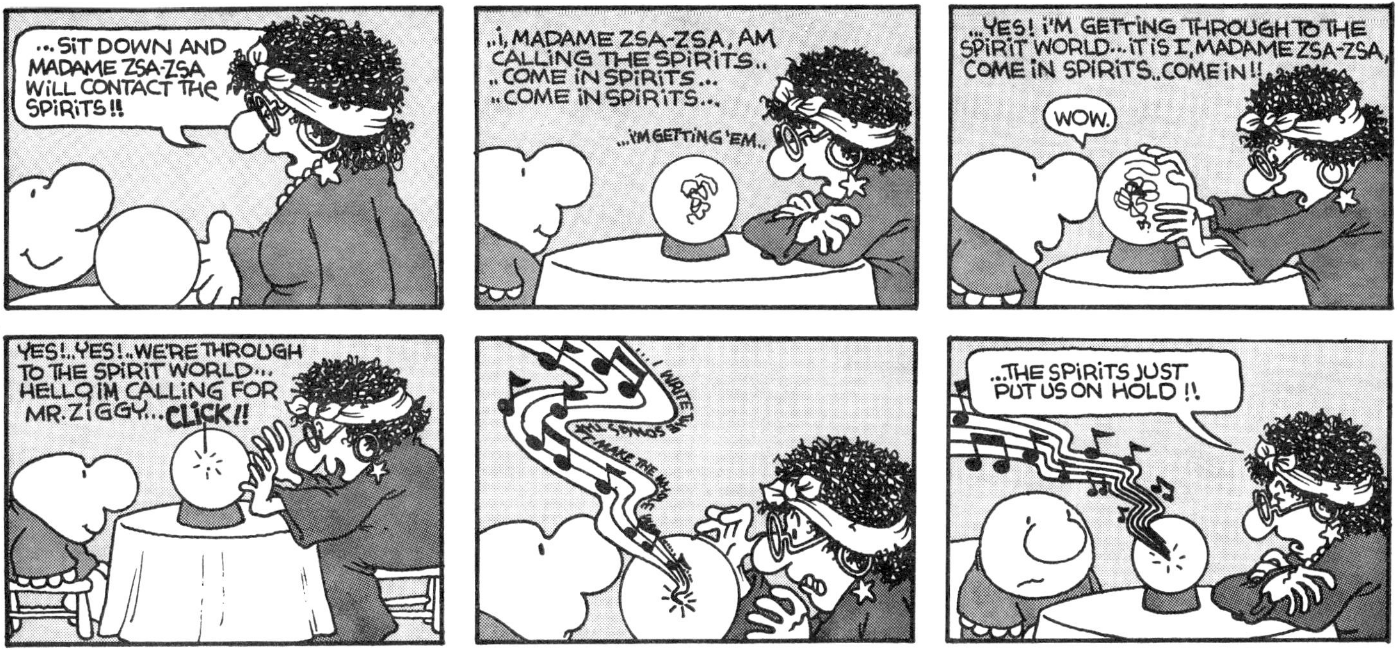
...SIT DOWN AND MADAME ZSA-ZSA WILL CONTACT THE SPIRITS!!
...I, MADAME ZSA-ZSA, AM CALLING THE SPIRITS.. ..COME IN SPIRITS... ..COME IN SPIRITS...
...I'M GETTING 'EM..
...YES! I'M GETTING THROUGH TO THE SPIRIT WORLD...IT IS I, MADAME ZSA-ZSA, COME IN SPIRITS..COME IN!!
WOW.
YES!..YES!..WE'RE THROUGH TO THE SPIRIT WORLD... HELLO IM CALLING FOR MR. ZIGGY...CLICK!!
...I WRITE THE SONGS THAT MAKE THE WHOLE WORLD.....
...THE SPIRITS JUST PUT US ON HOLD!!

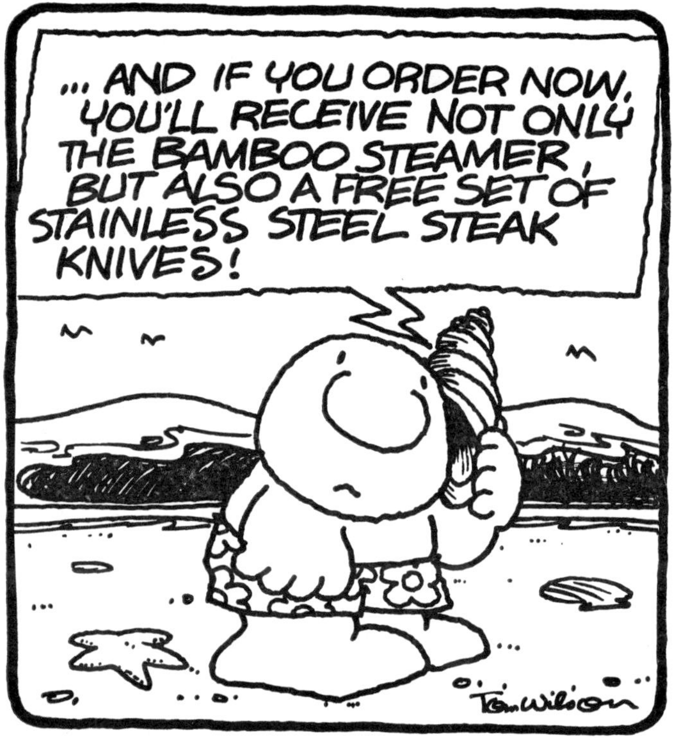
...AND IF YOU ORDER NOW, YOU'LL RECEIVE NOT ONLY THE BAMBOO STEAMER, BUT ALSO A FREE SET OF STAINLESS STEEL STEAK KNIVES!
Tom Wilson

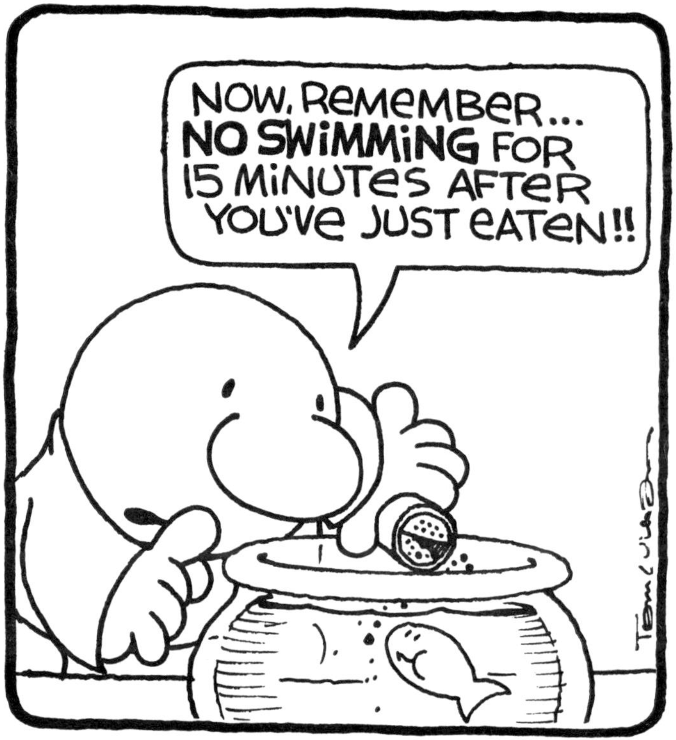
NOW, REMEMBER... NO SWIMMING FOR 15 MINUTES AFTER YOU'VE JUST EATEN!!
Tom Wilson

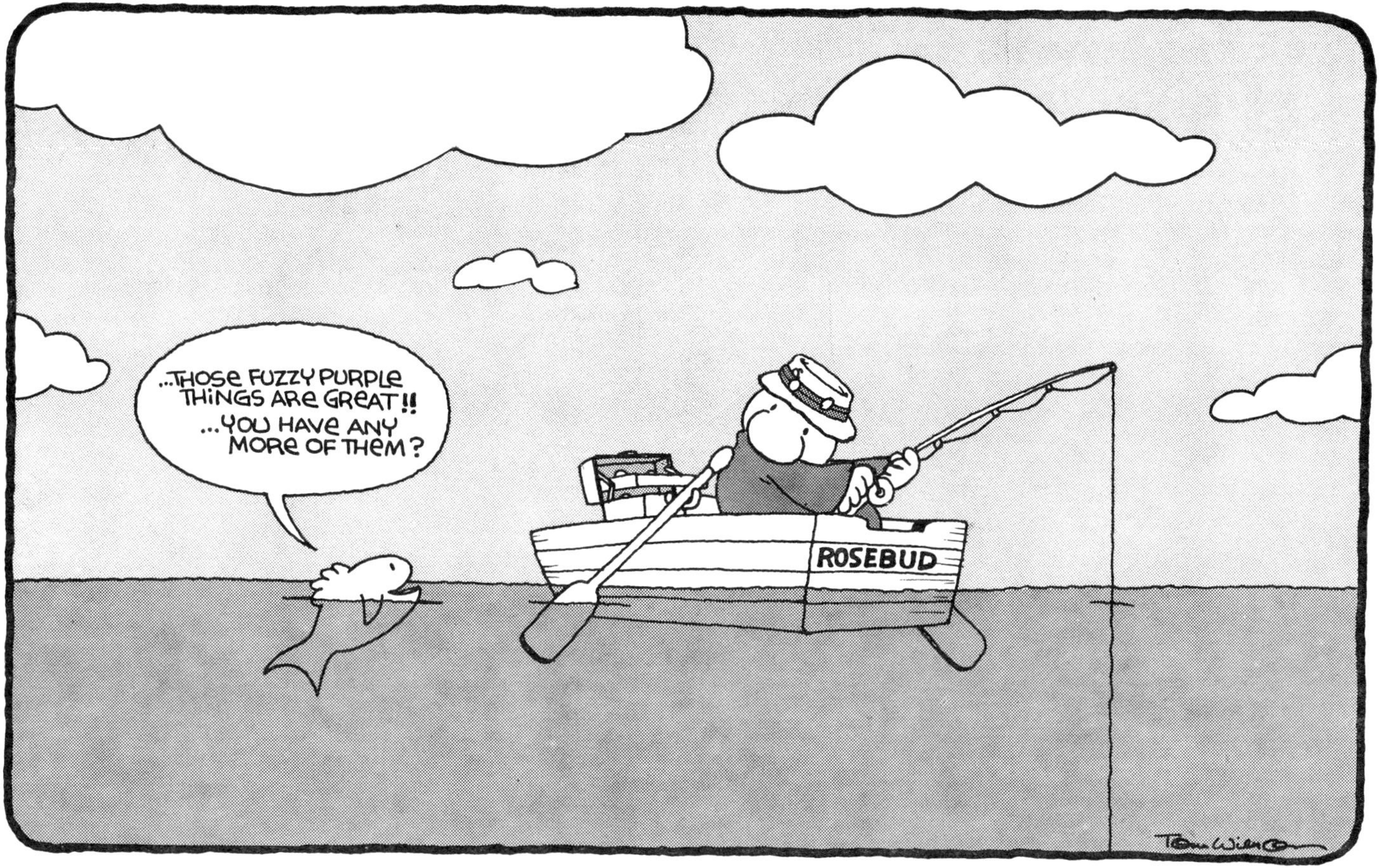
...THOSE FUZZY PURPLE THINGS ARE GREAT!! ...YOU HAVE ANY MORE OF THEM?
ROSEBUD

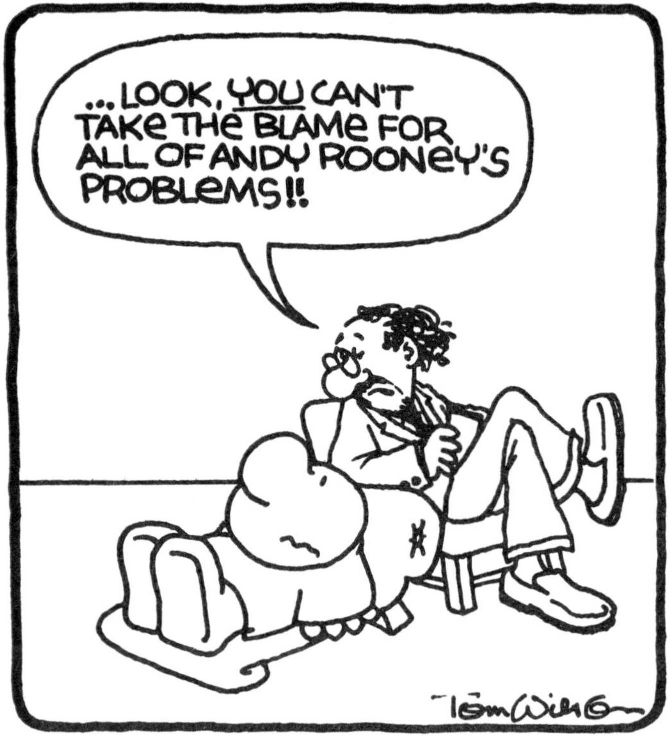
...LOOK, YOU CAN'T TAKE THE BLAME FOR ALL OF ANDY ROONEY'S PROBLEMS!!
Tom Wilson

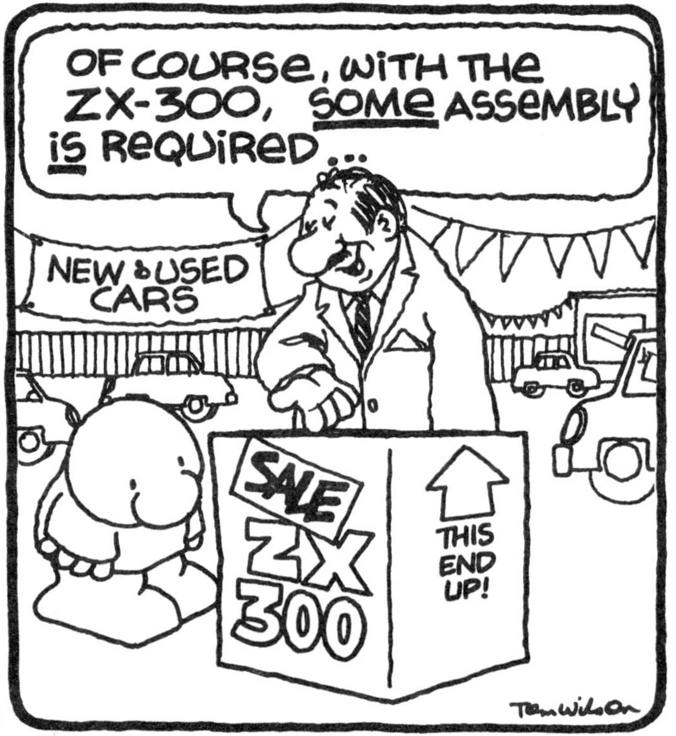
OF COURSE, WITH THE ZX-300, SOME ASSEMBLY IS REQUIRED...
NEW & USED CARS
SALE
ZX 300
THIS END UP!
Tom Wilson

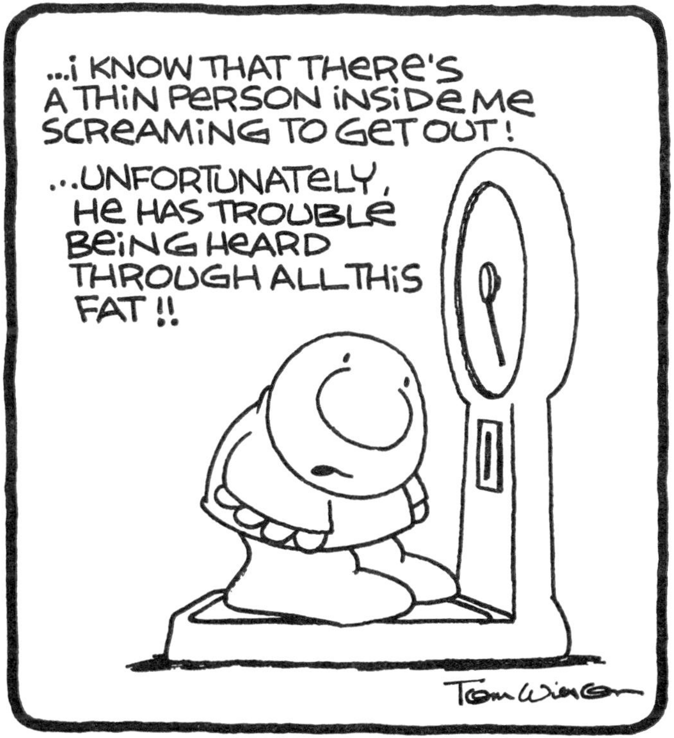
...I KNOW THAT THERE'S A THIN PERSON INSIDE ME SCREAMING TO GET OUT!
...UNFORTUNATELY, HE HAS TROUBLE BEING HEARD THROUGH ALL THIS FAT!!
Tom Wilson

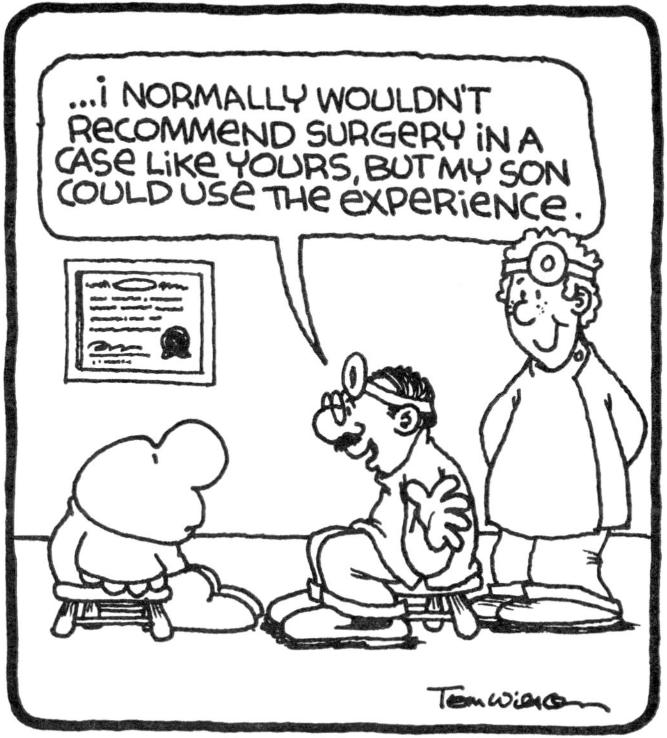
...I NORMALLY WOULDN'T RECOMMEND SURGERY IN A CASE LIKE YOURS, BUT MY SON COULD USE THE EXPERIENCE.
Tom Wilson

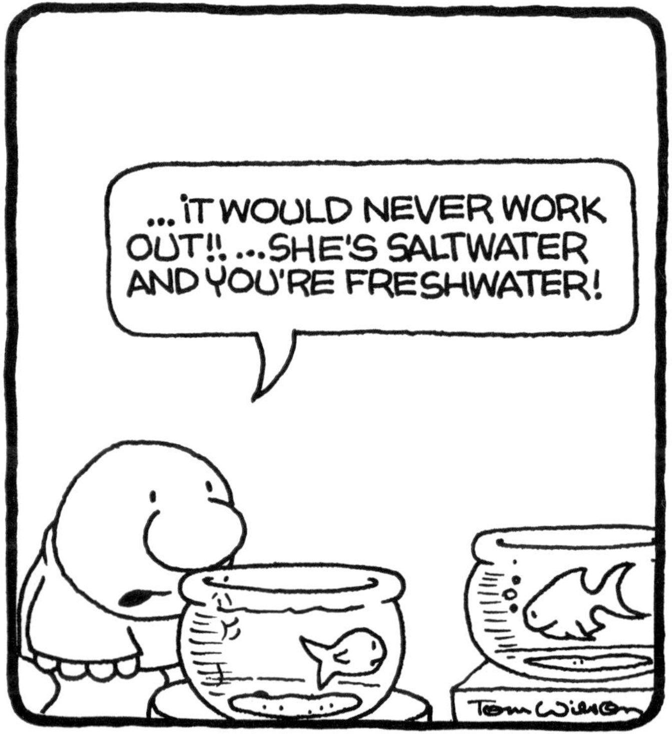
...IT WOULD NEVER WORK OUT!! ...SHE'S SALTWATER AND YOU'RE FRESHWATER!

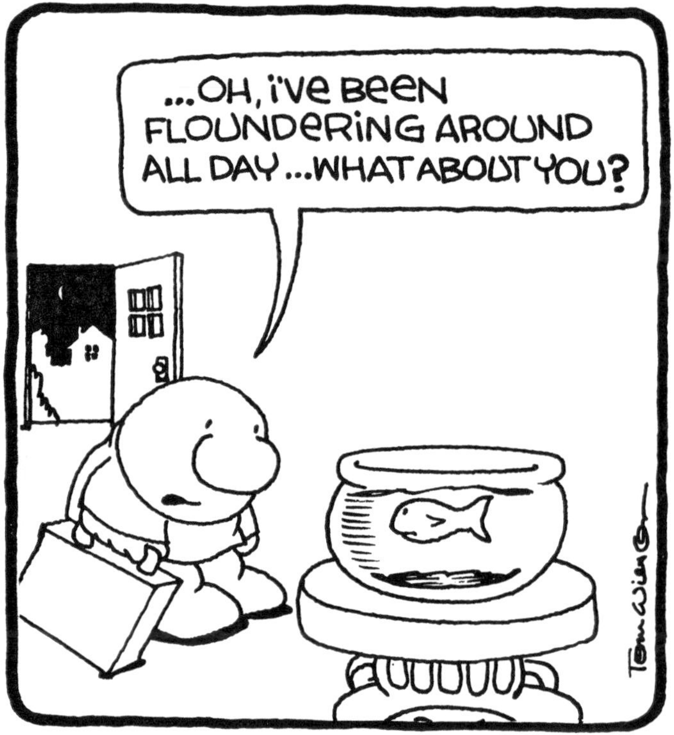
...OH, I'VE BEEN FLOUNDERING AROUND ALL DAY ...WHAT ABOUT YOU?

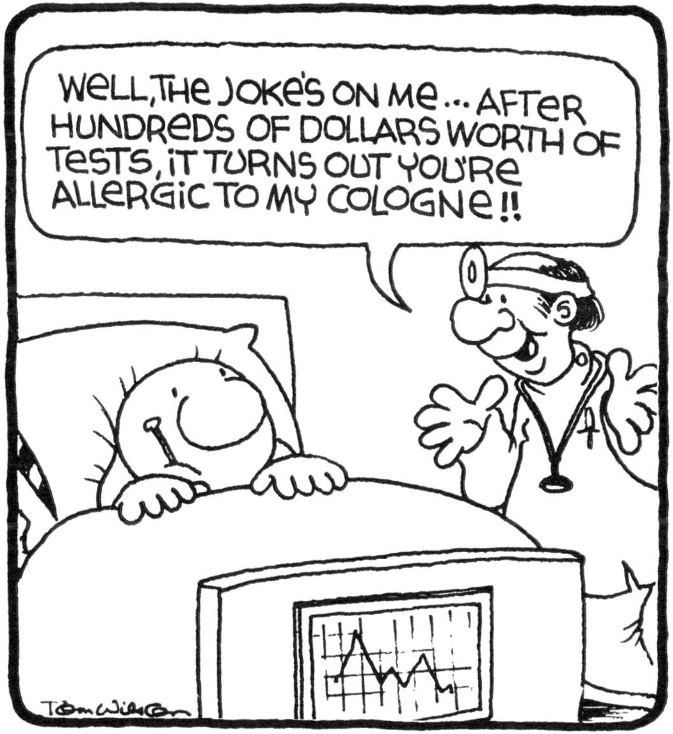
WELL, THE JOKE'S ON ME... AFTER HUNDREDS OF DOLLARS WORTH OF TESTS, IT TURNS OUT YOU'RE ALLERGIC TO MY COLOGNE!!
Tom Wilson

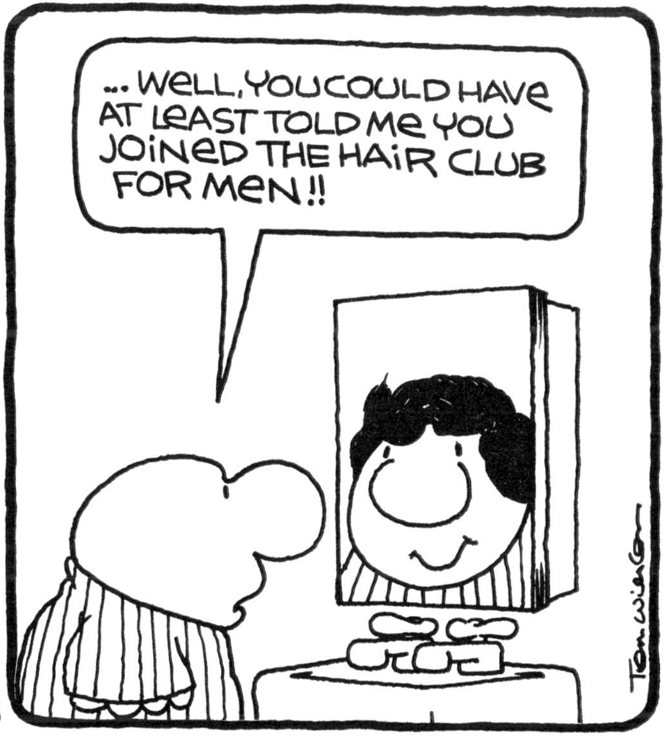
...WELL, YOU COULD HAVE AT LEAST TOLD ME YOU JOINED THE HAIR CLUB FOR MEN!!
Tom Wilson

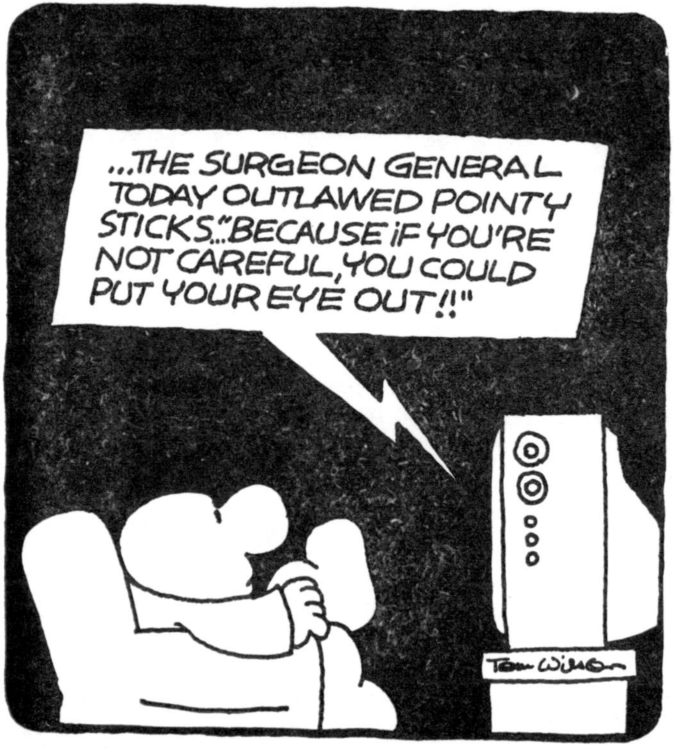
...THE SURGEON GENERAL TODAY OUTLAWED POINTY STICKS..."BECAUSE IF YOU'RE NOT CAREFUL, YOU COULD PUT YOUR EYE OUT!!"
Tom Wilson

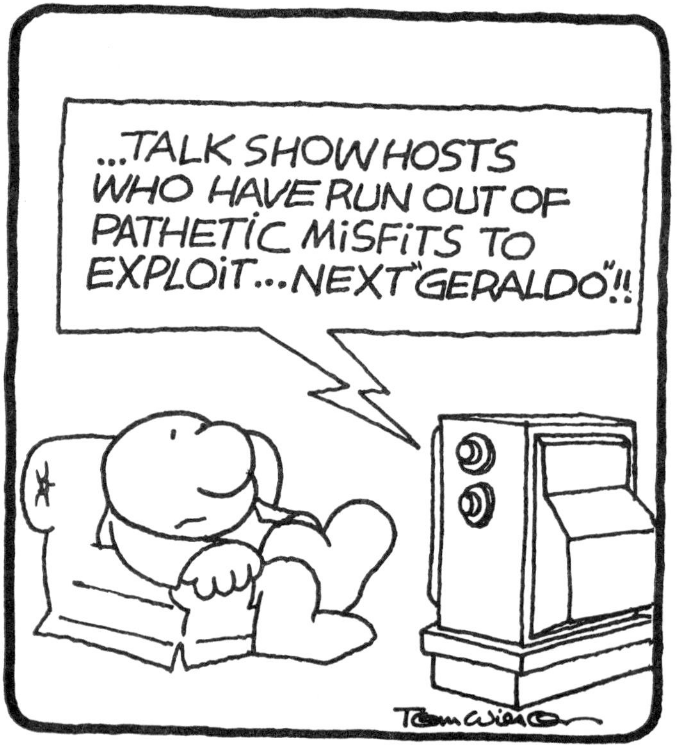
...TALK SHOW HOSTS WHO HAVE RUN OUT OF PATHETIC MISFITS TO EXPLOIT...NEXT "GERALDO"!!
Tom Wilson

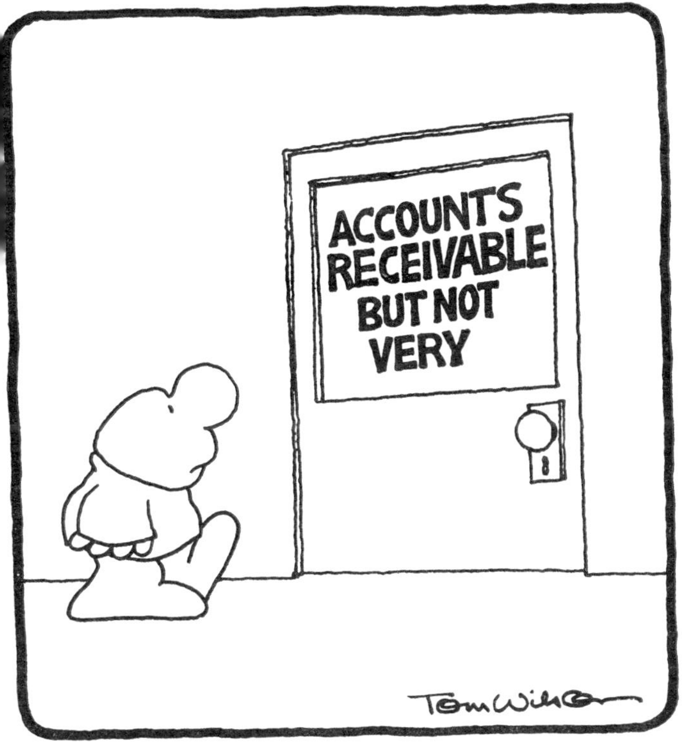
ACCOUNTS RECEIVABLE BUT NOT VERY
Tom Wilson

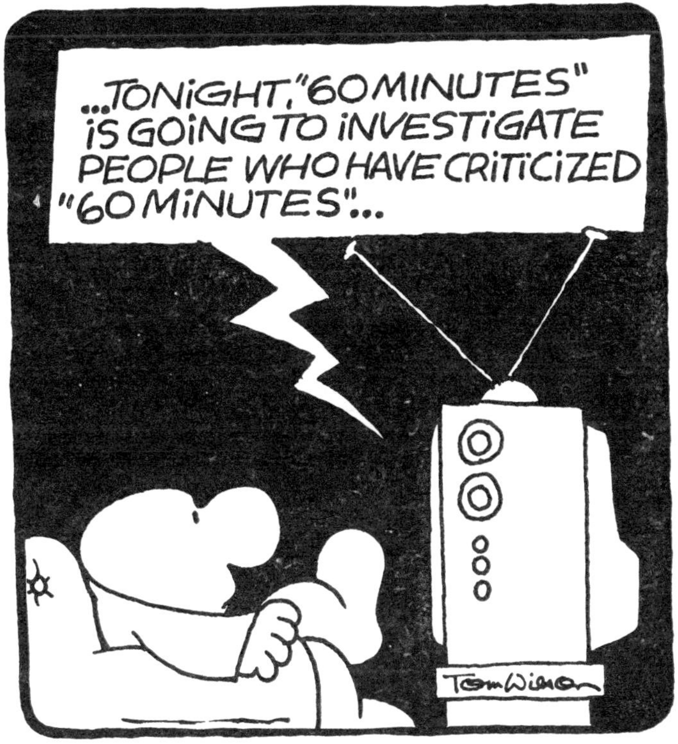
...TONIGHT, "60 MINUTES" IS GOING TO INVESTIGATE PEOPLE WHO HAVE CRITICIZED "60 MINUTES"...
Tom Wilson

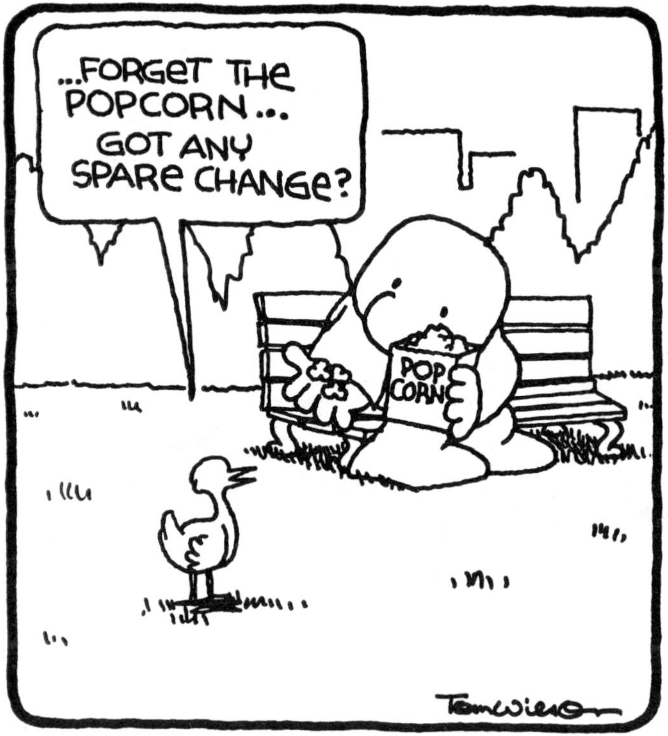
...FORGET THE POPCORN... GOT ANY SPARE CHANGE?
POP CORN
Tom Wilson

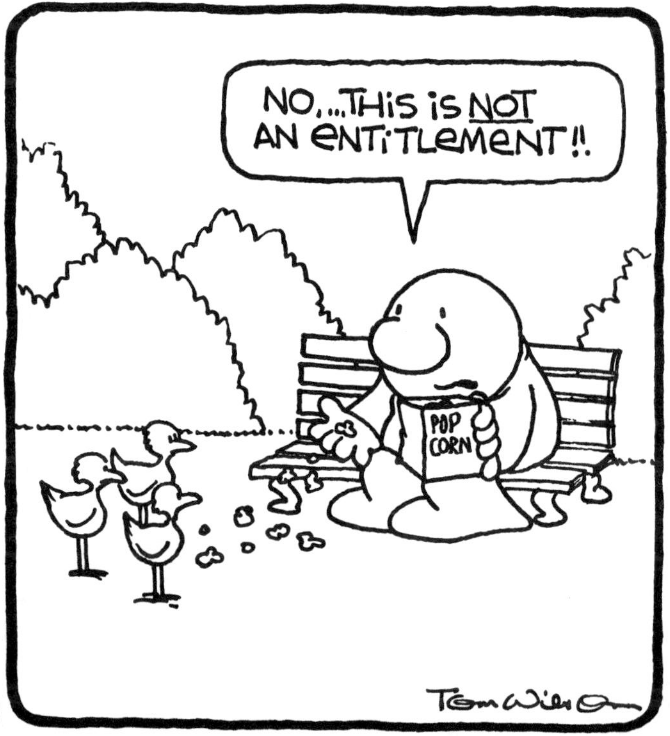
NO,...THIS IS NOT AN ENTITLEMENT!!
POP CORN
Tom Wilson

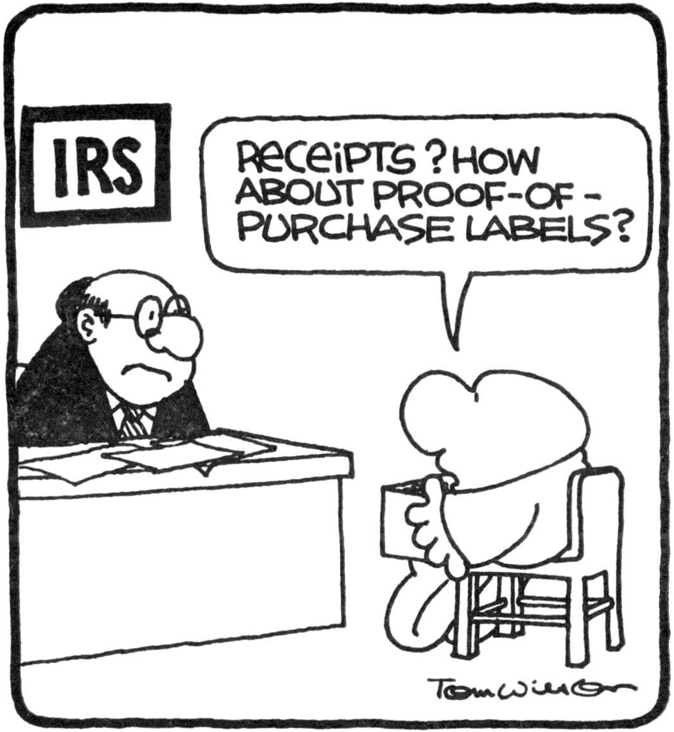
IRS
RECEIPTS? HOW ABOUT PROOF-OF-PURCHASE LABELS?

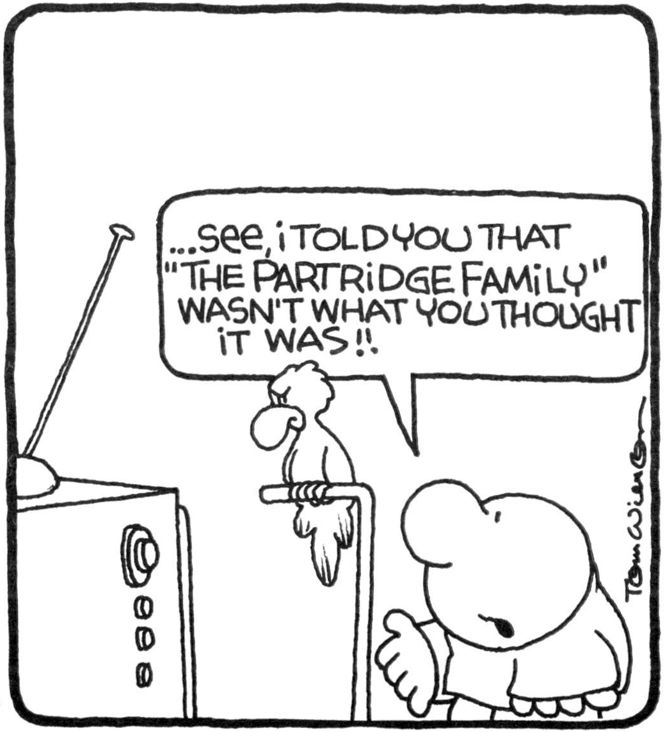
...SEE, I TOLD YOU THAT "THE PARTRIDGE FAMILY" WASN'T WHAT YOU THOUGHT IT WAS!!

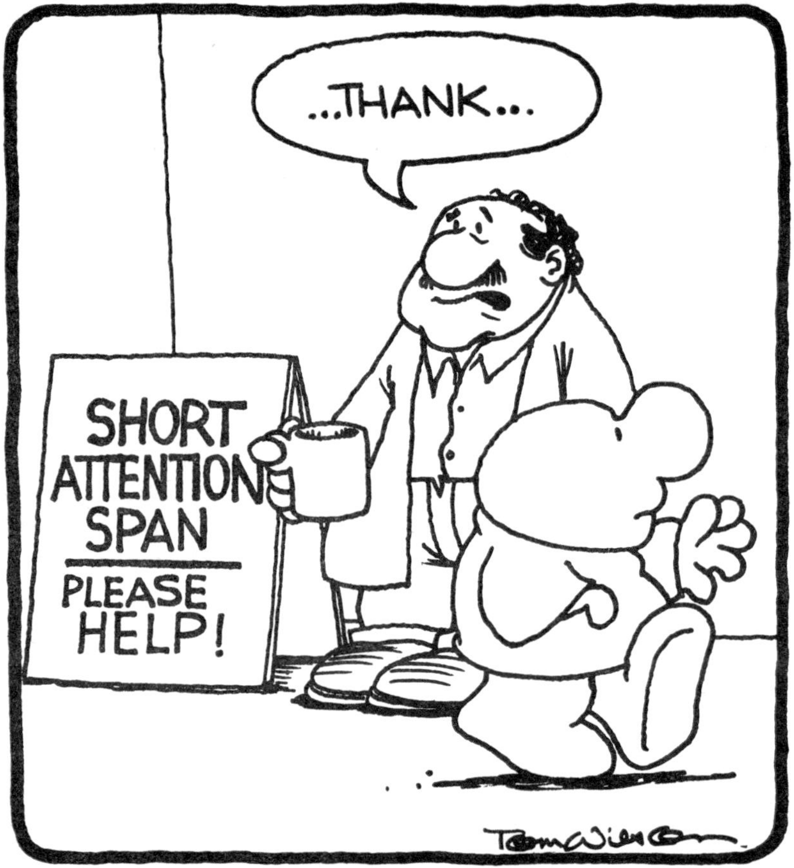

...THANK...
SHORT ATTENTION SPAN
PLEASE HELP!

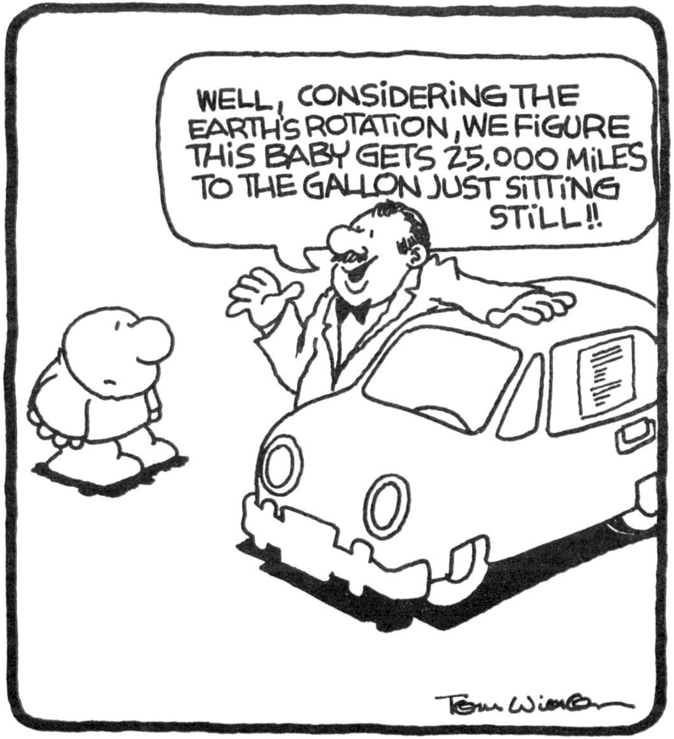
WELL, CONSIDERING THE EARTH'S ROTATION, WE FIGURE THIS BABY GETS 25,000 MILES TO THE GALLON JUST SITTING STILL!!
TOM WILSON

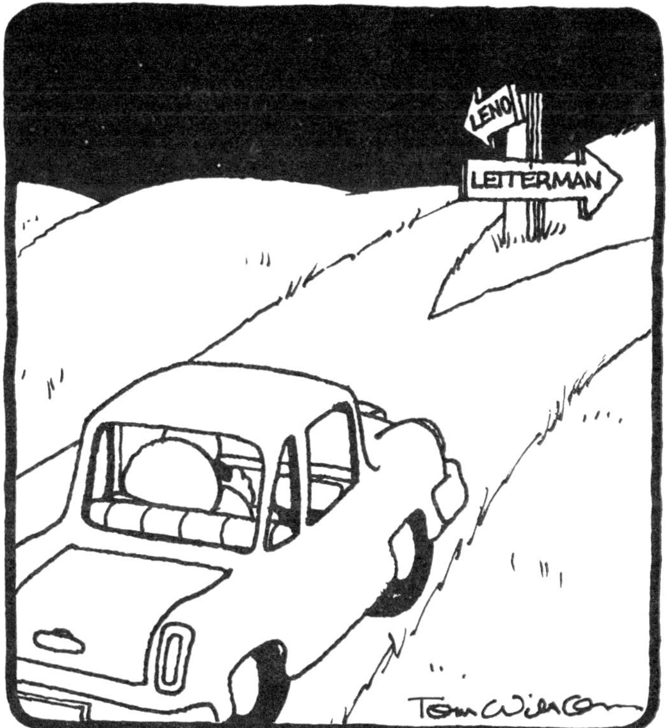
LENO
LETTERMAN
TOM WILSON

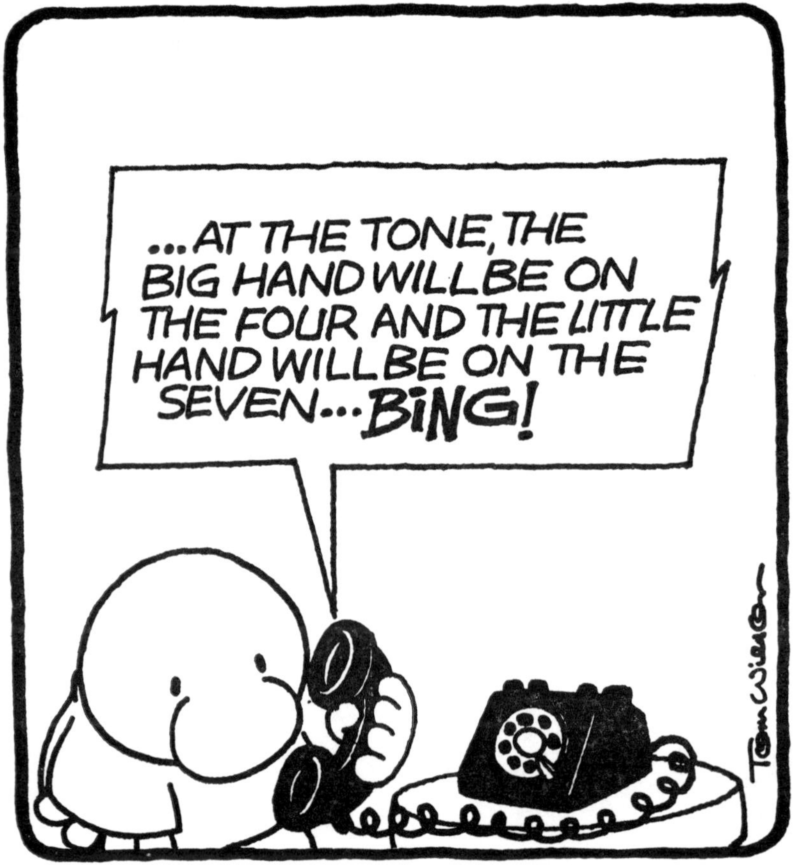
...AT THE TONE, THE BIG HAND WILL BE ON THE FOUR AND THE LITTLE HAND WILL BE ON THE SEVEN...BING!
TOM WILSON

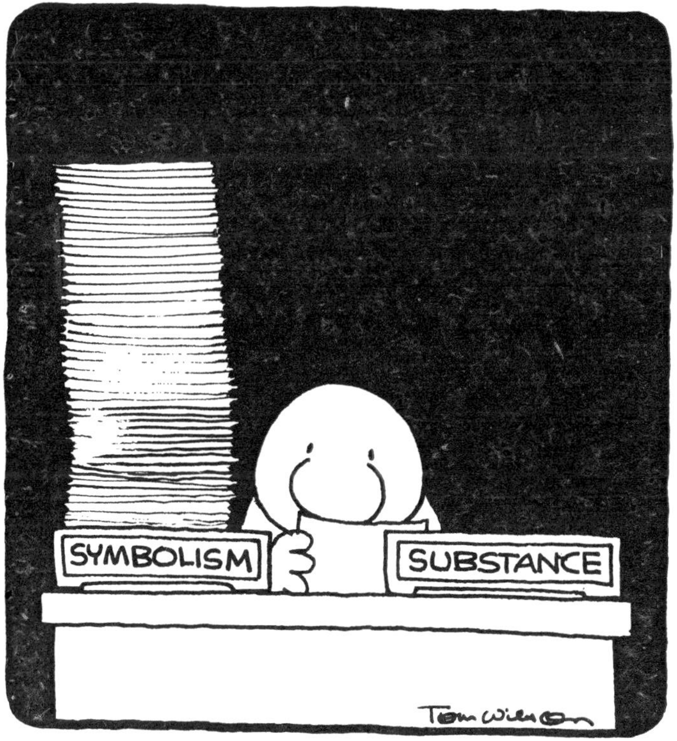
SYMBOLISM
SUBSTANCE
Tom Wilson

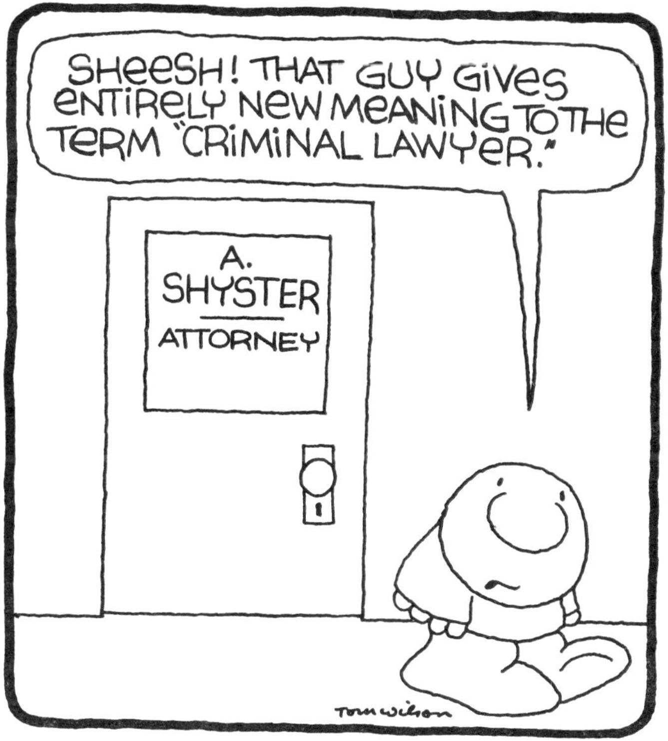
SHEESH! THAT GUY GIVES ENTIRELY NEW MEANING TO THE TERM "CRIMINAL LAWYER."
A. SHYSTER
ATTORNEY
Tom Wilson

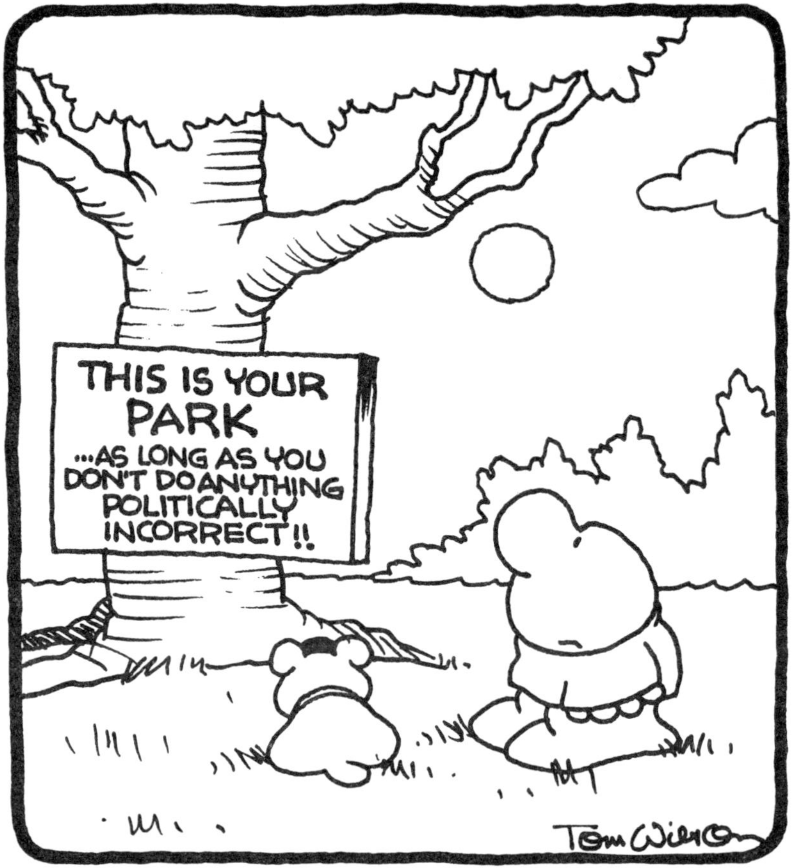
THIS IS YOUR PARK
...AS LONG AS YOU DON'T DO ANYTHING POLITICALLY INCORRECT!!
TOM WILSON

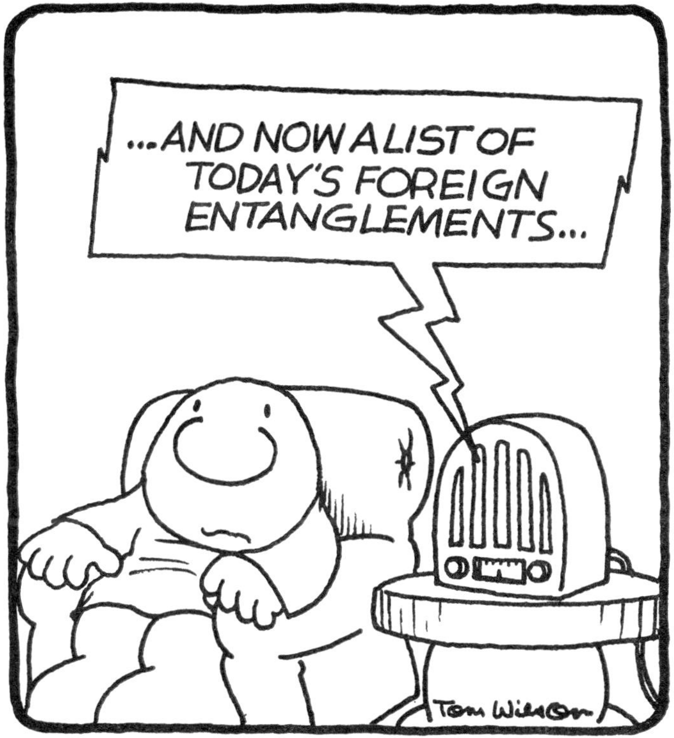
...AND NOW A LIST OF TODAY'S FOREIGN ENTANGLEMENTS...

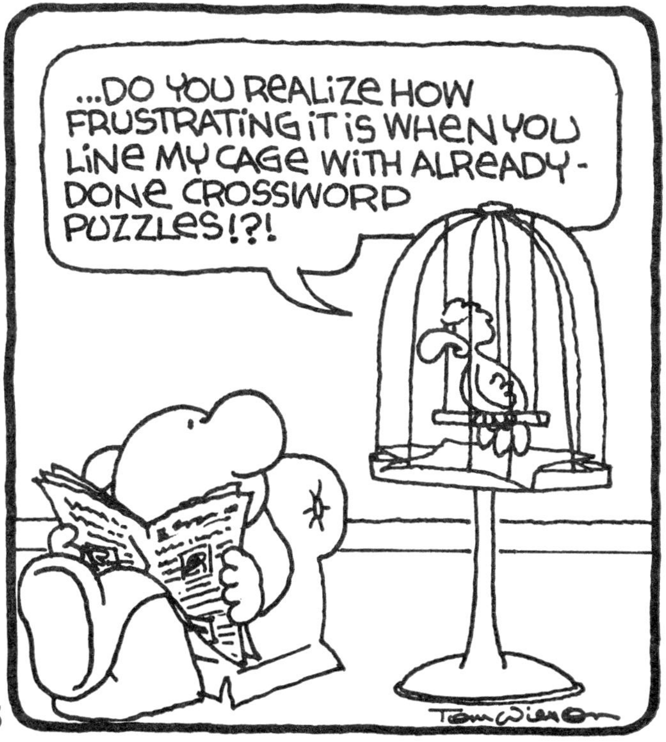
...DO YOU REALIZE HOW FRUSTRATING IT IS WHEN YOU LINE MY CAGE WITH ALREADY-DONE CROSSWORD PUZZLES!?!

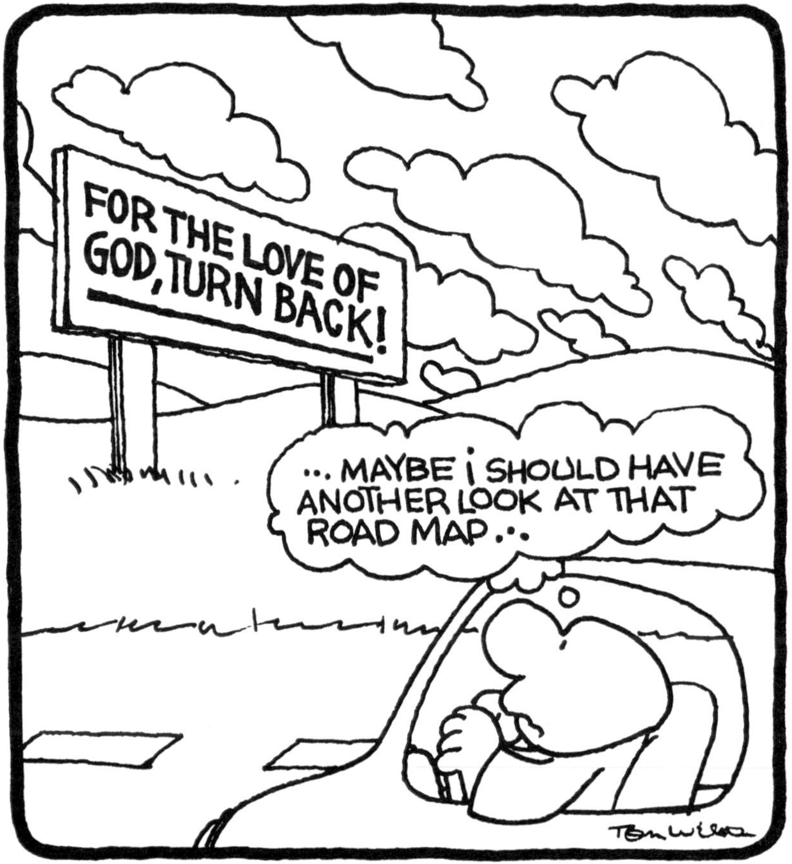
FOR THE LOVE OF GOD, TURN BACK!
... MAYBE i SHOULD HAVE ANOTHER LOOK AT THAT ROAD MAP...

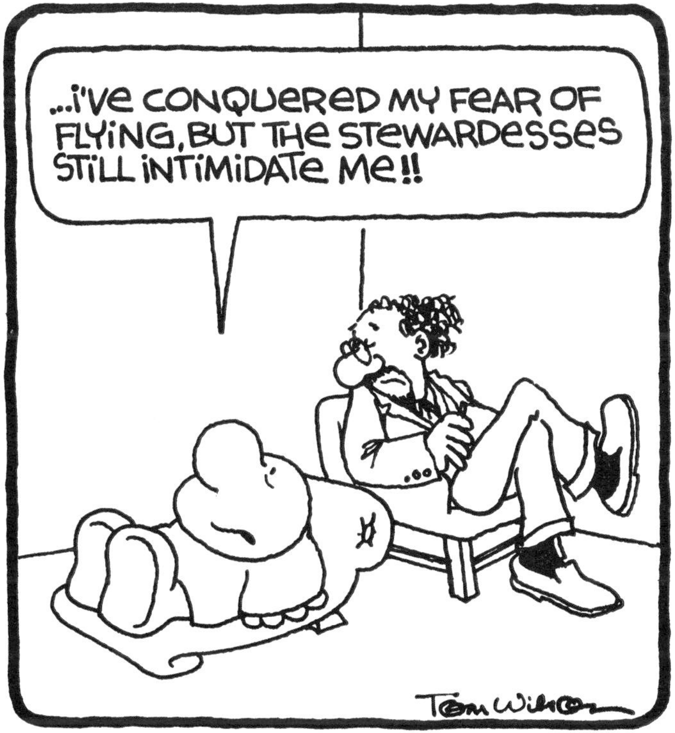
...i'VE CONQUERED MY FEAR OF FLYiNG, BUT THE STEWARDESSES STiLL iNTiMiDATE ME!!
Tom Wilson

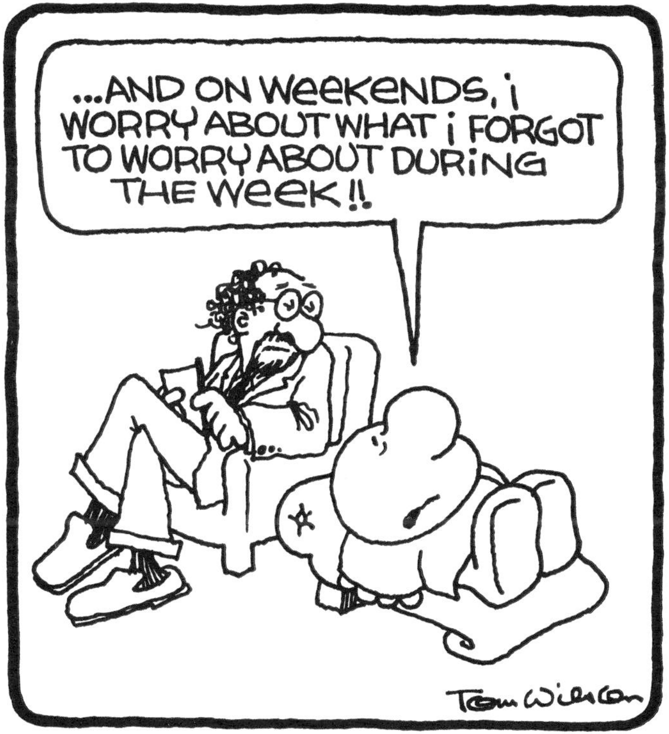
...AND ON WEEKENDS, i WORRY ABOUT WHAT i FORGOT TO WORRY ABOUT DURiNG THE WEEK!!
Tom Wilson

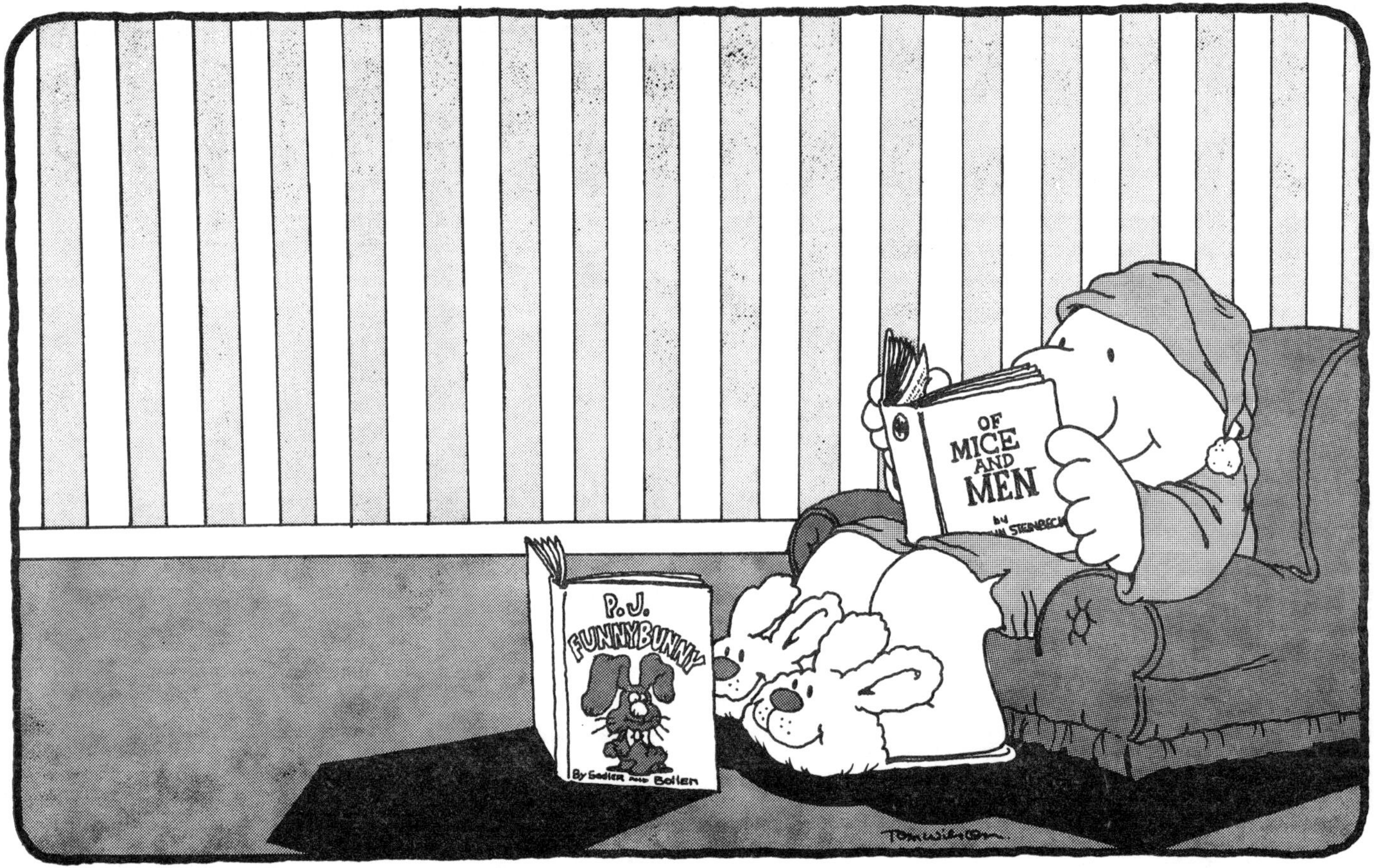
OF MICE AND MEN
by
STEINBECK
P.J. FUNNYBUNNY
By Sadler and Bollen
Tom Wilson

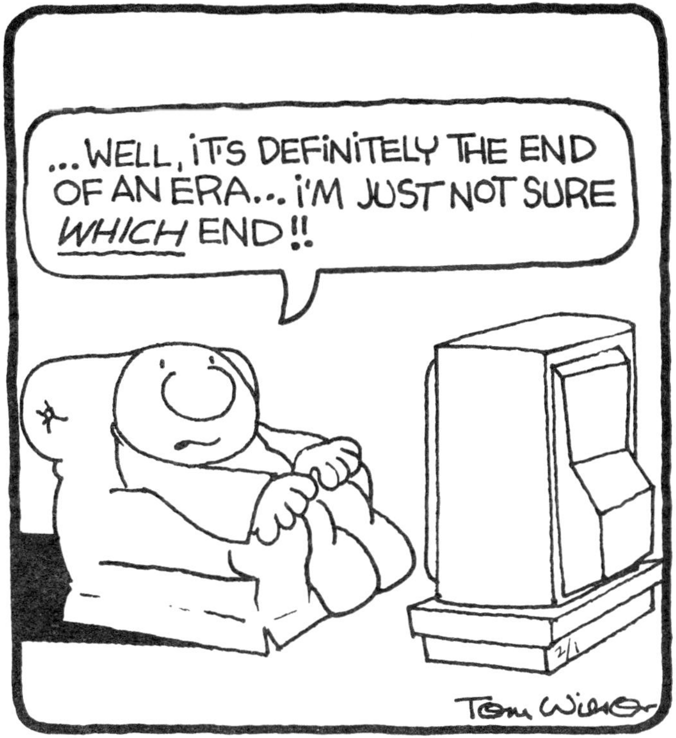
...WELL, IT'S DEFINITELY THE END OF AN ERA... I'M JUST NOT SURE WHICH END!!
TOM WILSON

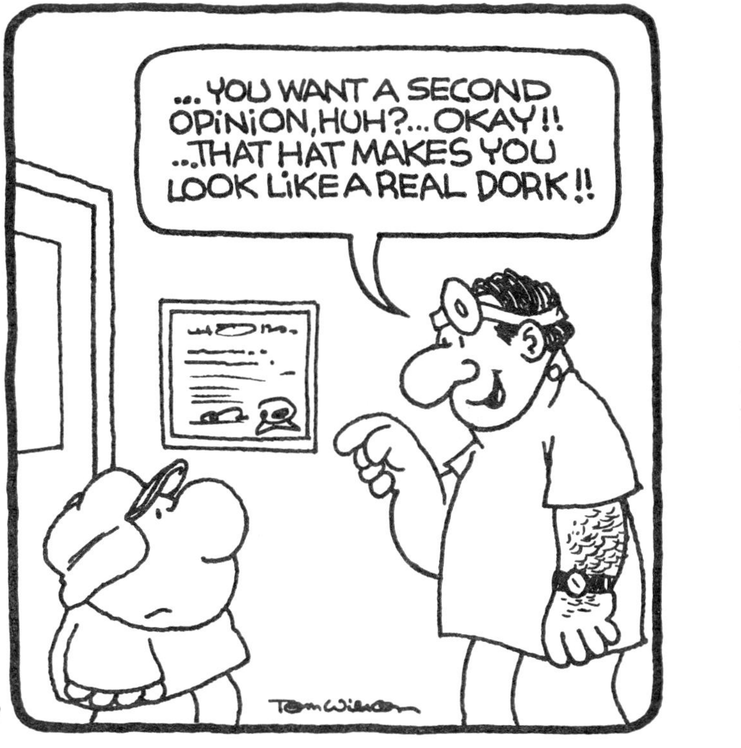
...YOU WANT A SECOND OPINION, HUH?... OKAY!! ...THAT HAT MAKES YOU LOOK LIKE A REAL DORK!!
TOM WILSON

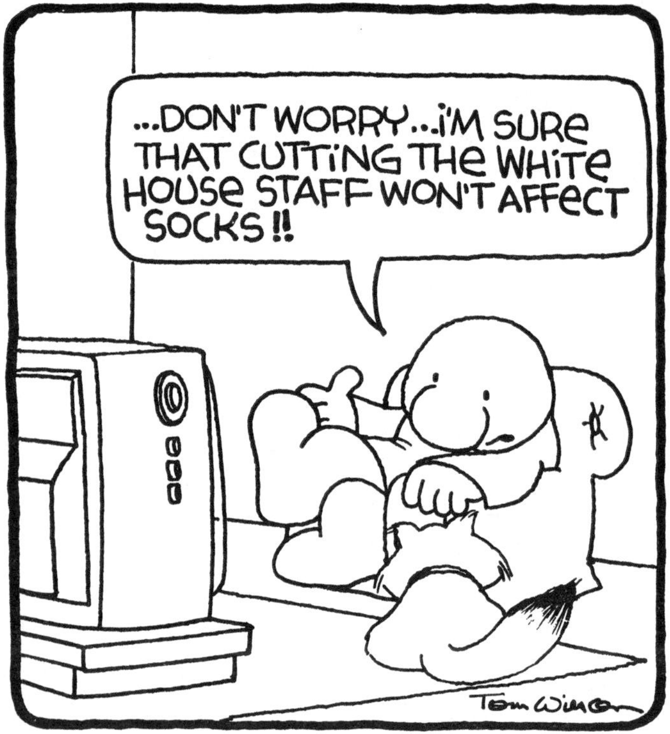
...DON'T WORRY...I'M SURE THAT CUTTING THE WHITE HOUSE STAFF WON'T AFFECT SOCKS !!
TOM WILSON

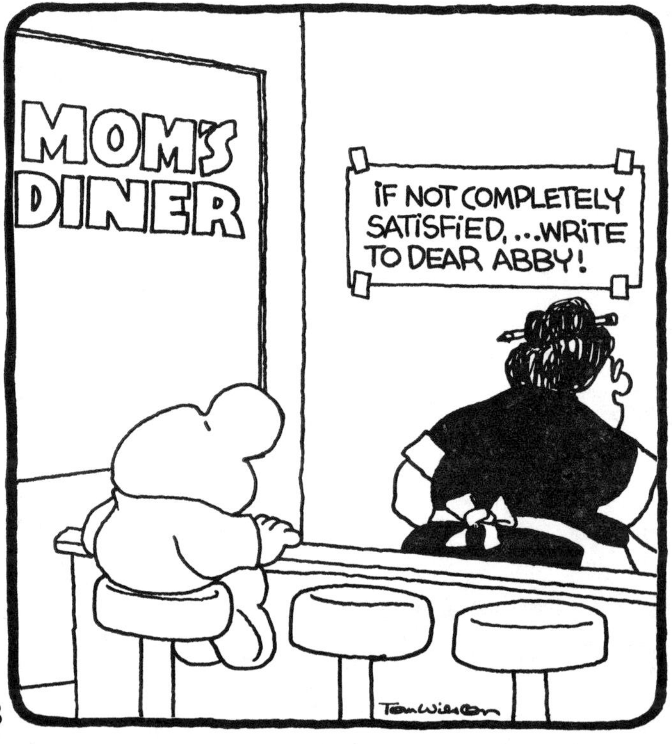
MOM'S DINER
IF NOT COMPLETELY SATISFIED, ...WRITE TO DEAR ABBY!
TOM WILSON

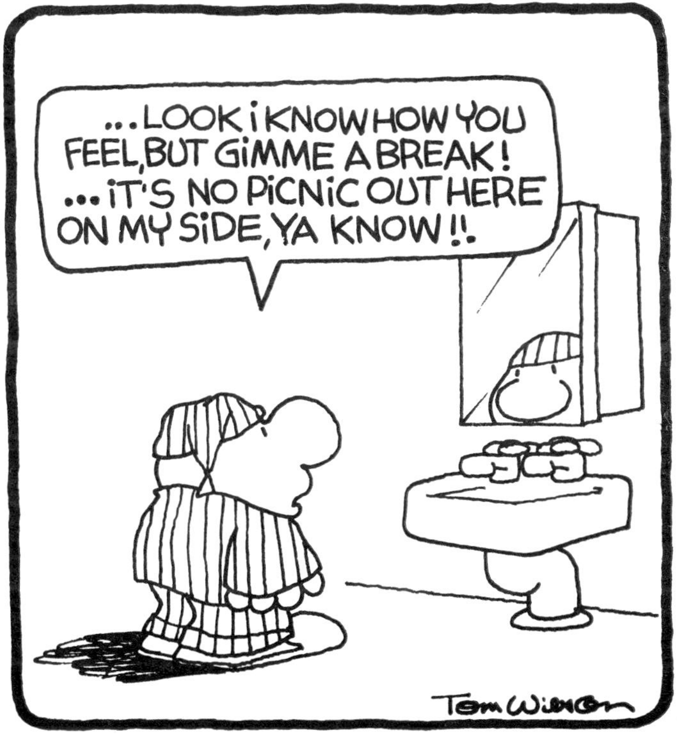
...LOOK i KNOW HOW YOU FEEL, BUT GiMME A BREAK! ...iT'S NO PiCNiC OUT HERE ON MY SiDE, YA KNOW!!.
Tom Wilson

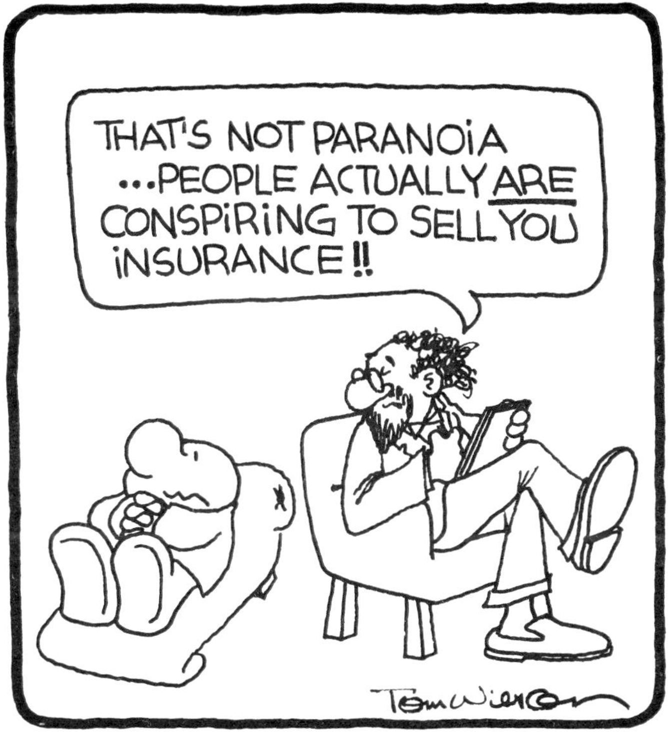
THAT'S NOT PARANOiA ...PEOPLE ACTUALLY ARE CONSPiRiNG TO SELL YOU iNSURANCE!!
Tom Wilson

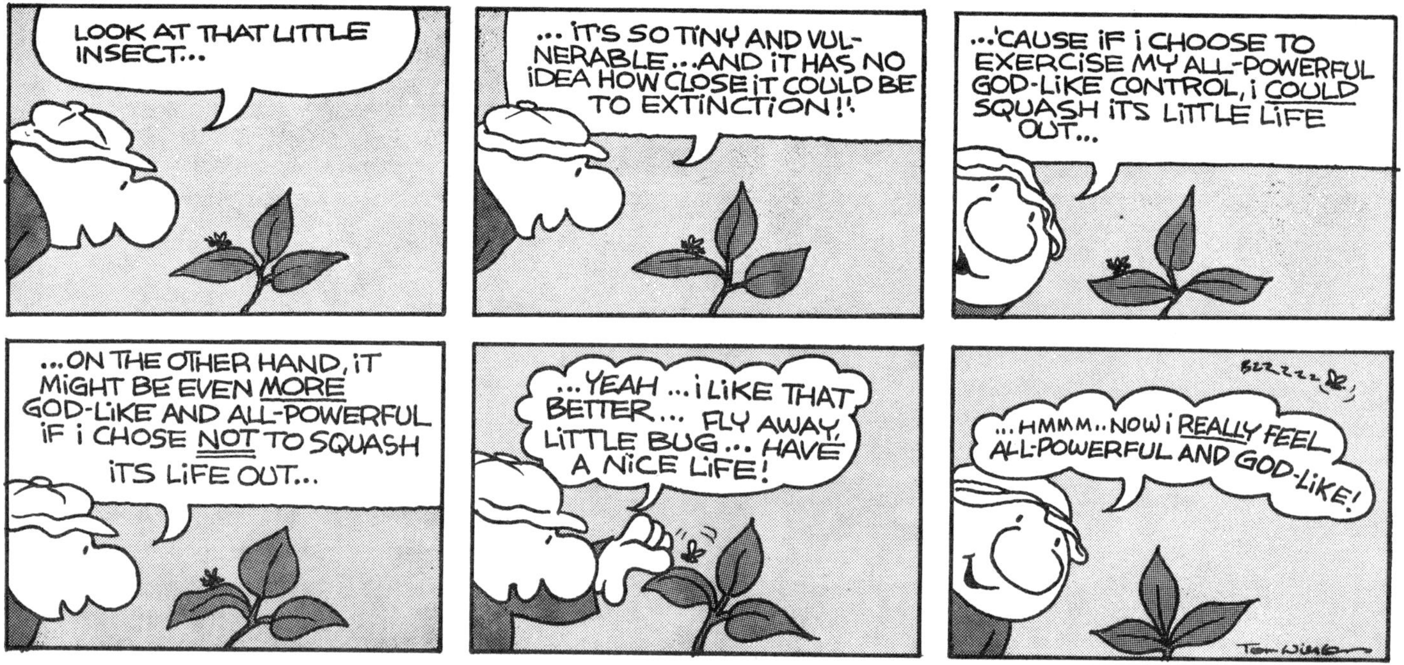
LOOK AT THAT LITTLE INSECT...
... IT'S SO TINY AND VULNERABLE... AND IT HAS NO IDEA HOW CLOSE IT COULD BE TO EXTINCTION!!
...'CAUSE IF I CHOOSE TO EXERCISE MY ALL-POWERFUL GOD-LIKE CONTROL, I COULD SQUASH ITS LITTLE LIFE OUT...
...ON THE OTHER HAND, IT MIGHT BE EVEN MORE GOD-LIKE AND ALL-POWERFUL IF I CHOSE NOT TO SQUASH ITS LIFE OUT...
...YEAH ...I LIKE THAT BETTER... FLY AWAY, LITTLE BUG... HAVE A NICE LIFE!
...HMMM..NOW I REALLY FEEL ALL-POWERFUL AND GOD-LIKE!

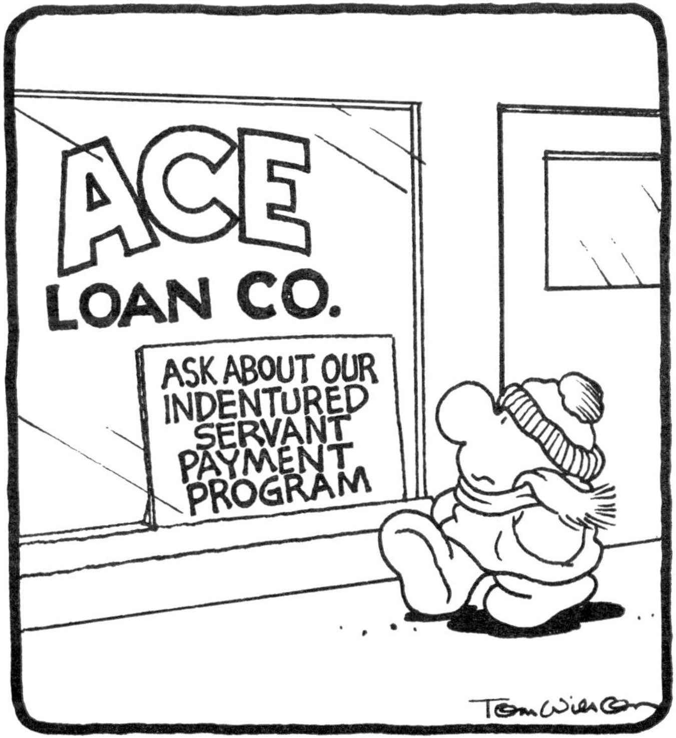
ACE
LOAN CO.
ASK ABOUT OUR INDENTURED SERVANT PAYMENT PROGRAM
TOM WILSON

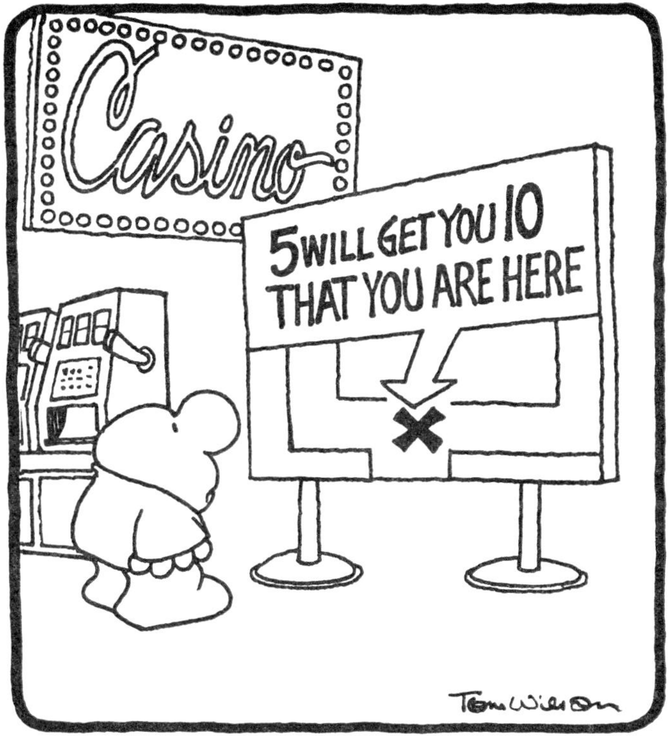
Casino
5 WILL GET YOU 10 THAT YOU ARE HERE
TOM WILSON

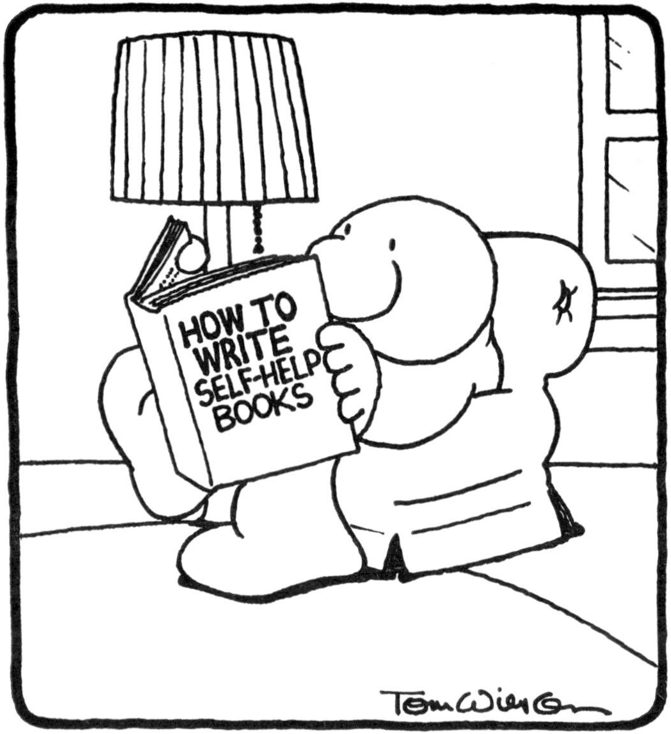
HOW TO WRITE SELF-HELP BOOKS
TOM WILSON

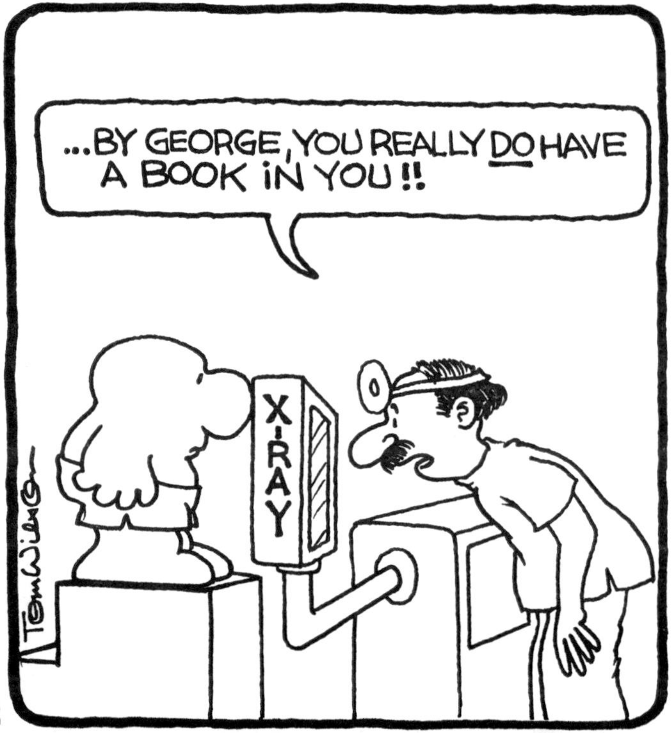
...BY GEORGE, YOU REALLY DO HAVE A BOOK IN YOU !!
X-RAY
TOM WILSON

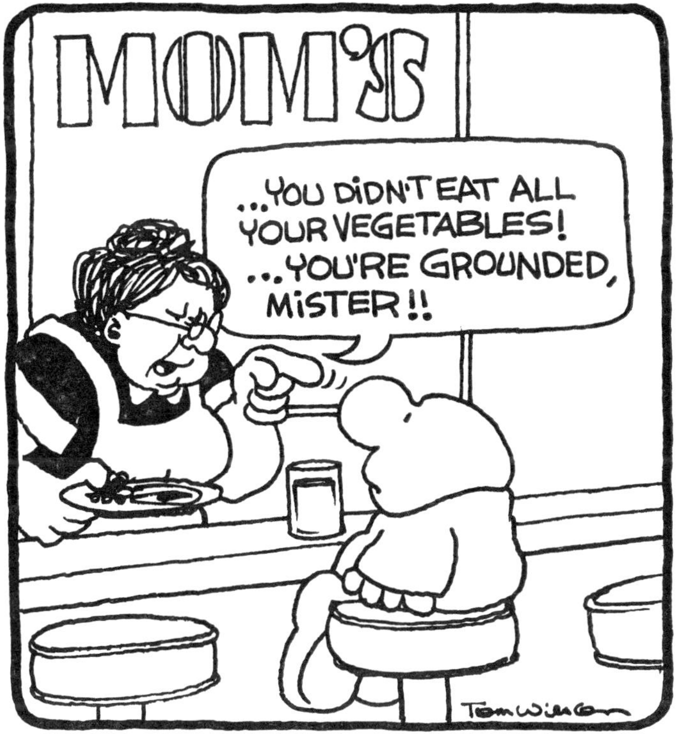
MOM'S
...YOU DIDN'T EAT ALL YOUR VEGETABLES! ...YOU'RE GROUNDED, MISTER!!
Tom Wilson

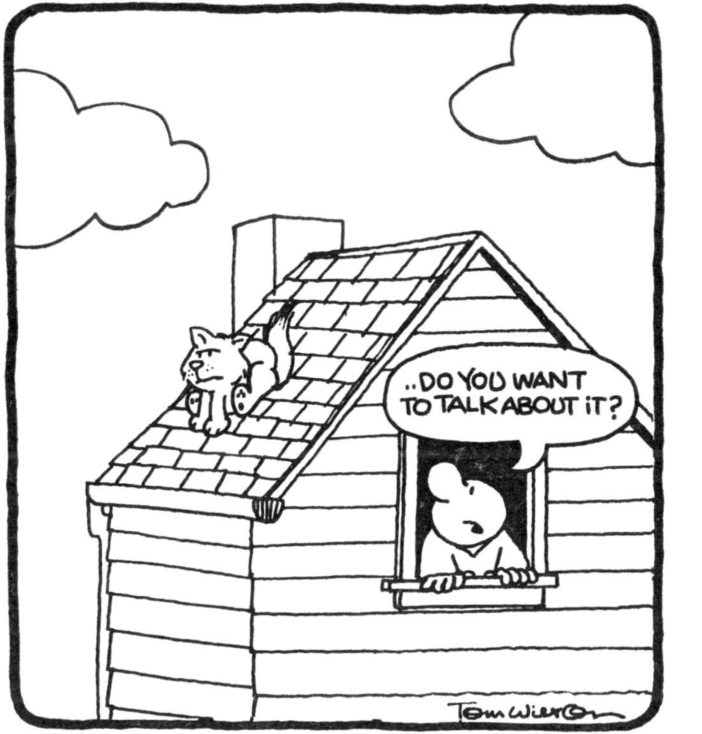
..DO YOU WANT TO TALK ABOUT IT?
Tom Wilson

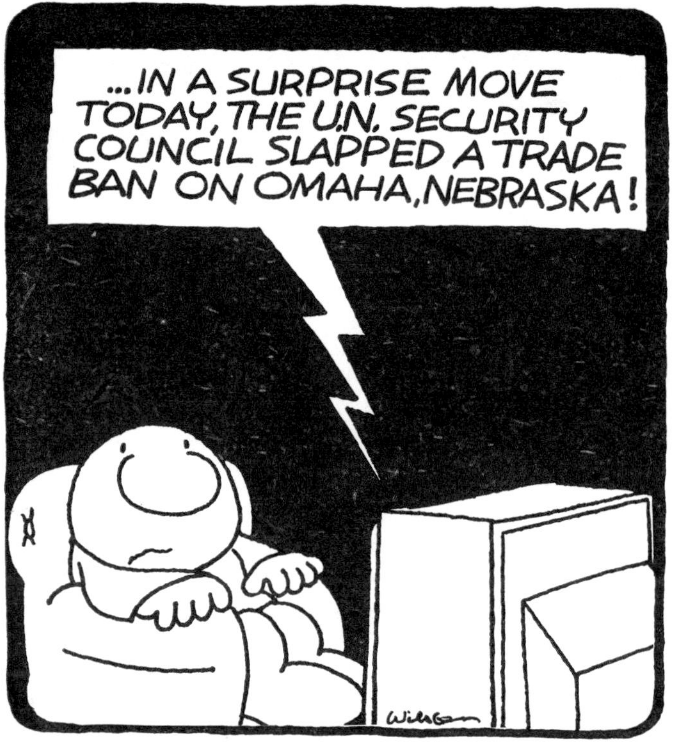
...IN A SURPRISE MOVE TODAY, THE U.N. SECURITY COUNCIL SLAPPED A TRADE BAN ON OMAHA, NEBRASKA!

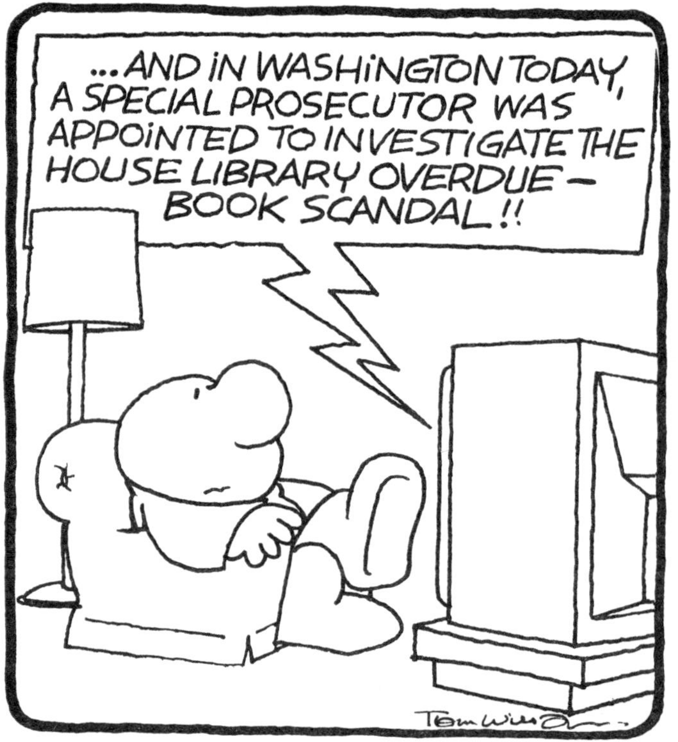
...AND IN WASHINGTON TODAY, A SPECIAL PROSECUTOR WAS APPOINTED TO INVESTIGATE THE HOUSE LIBRARY OVERDUE-BOOK SCANDAL!!

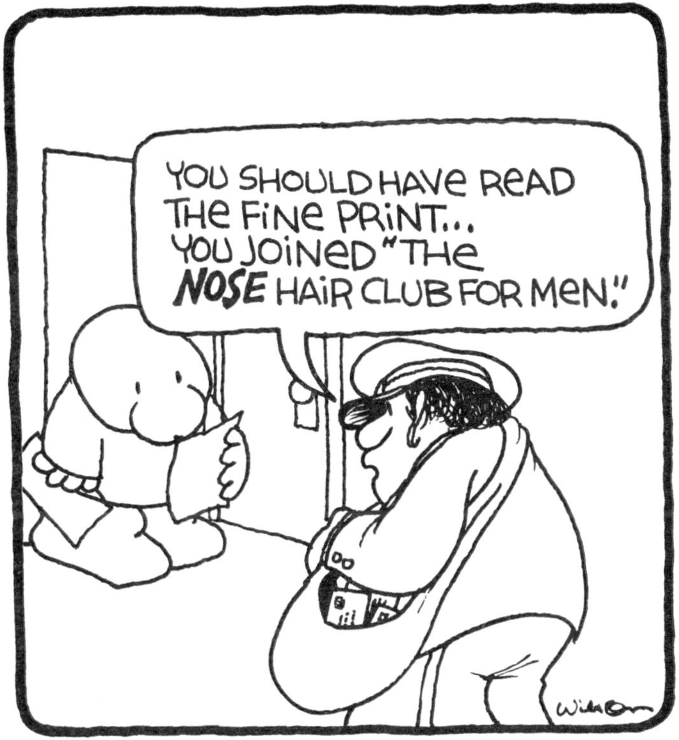
YOU SHOULD HAVE READ THE FINE PRINT... YOU JOINED "THE NOSE HAIR CLUB FOR MEN."
Wilson

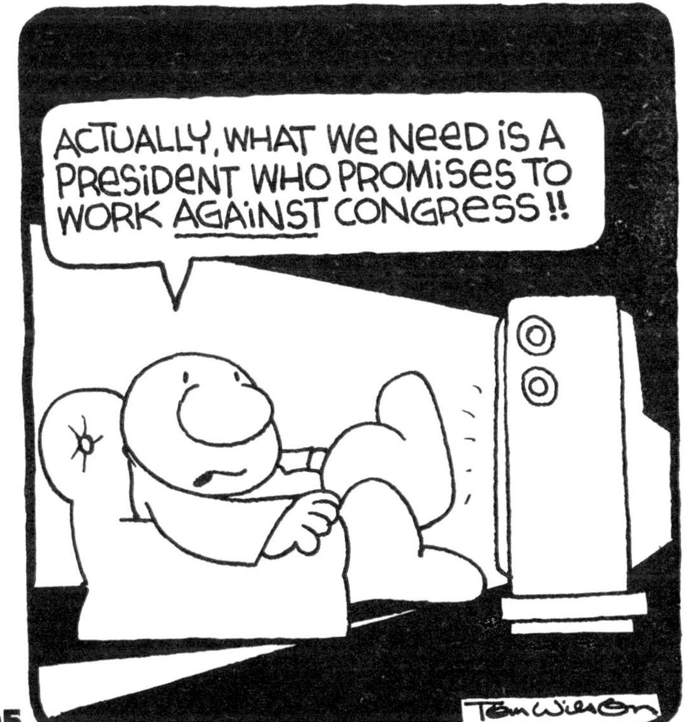
ACTUALLY, WHAT WE NEED IS A PRESIDENT WHO PROMISES TO WORK AGAINST CONGRESS !!
Tom Wilson

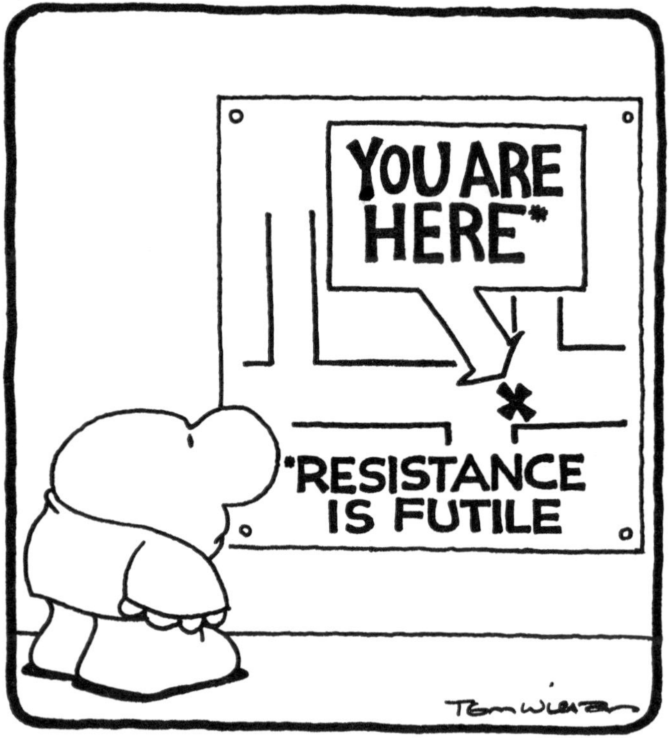
YOU ARE HERE*
*RESISTANCE IS FUTILE
TOM WILSON

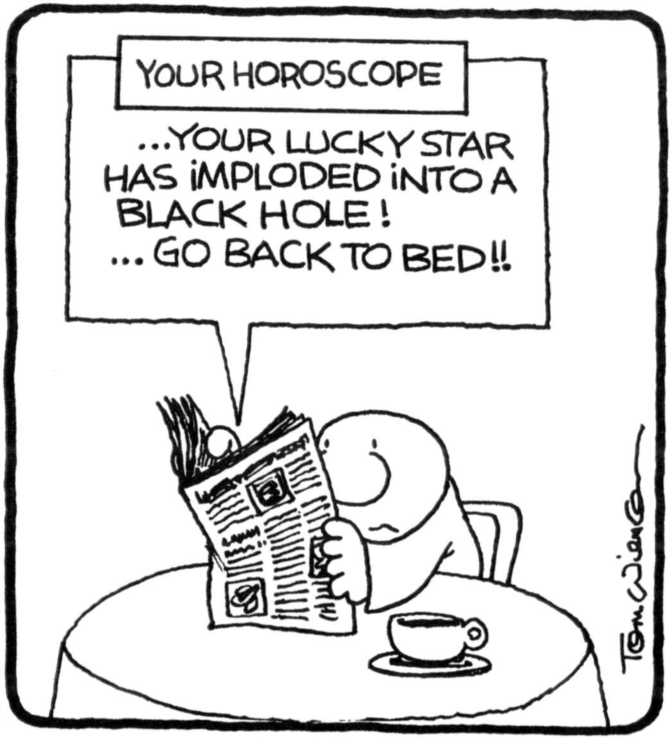
YOUR HOROSCOPE
...YOUR LUCKY STAR HAS IMPLODED INTO A BLACK HOLE! ...GO BACK TO BED!!
TOM WILSON

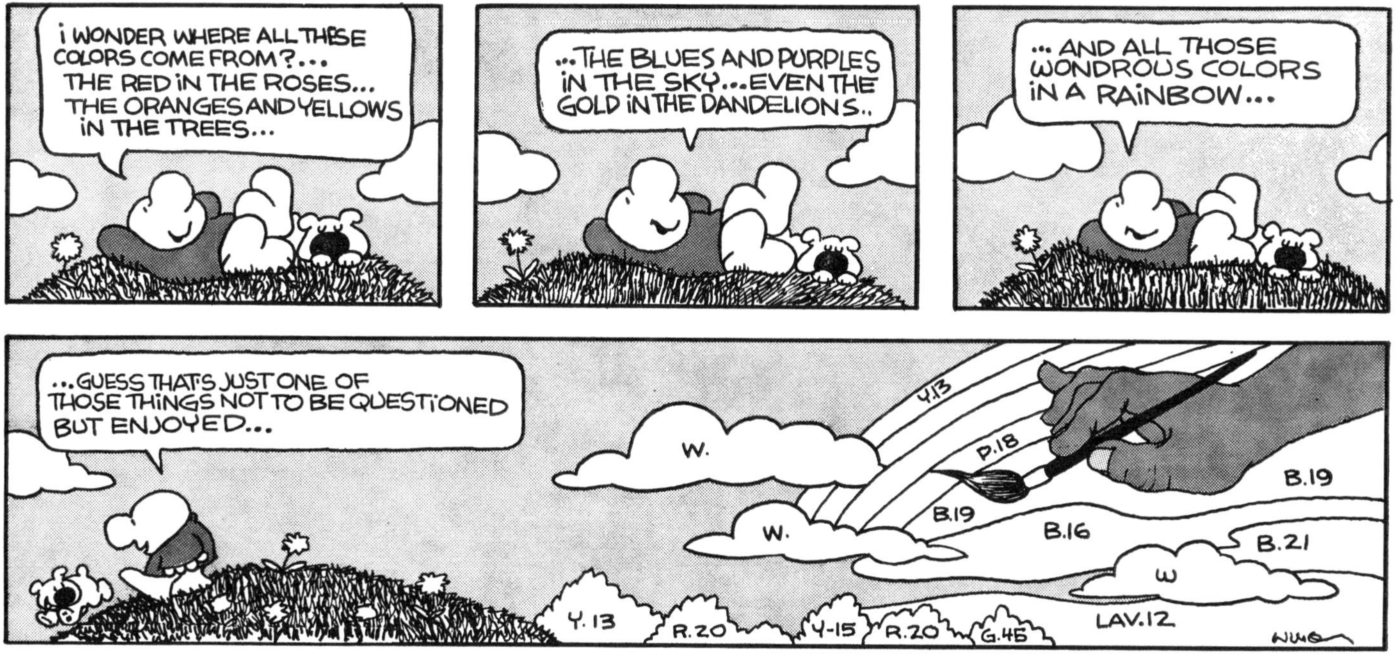
i WONDER WHERE ALL THESE COLORS COME FROM?... THE RED iN THE ROSES... THE ORANGES AND YELLOWS iN THE TREES...
...THE BLUES AND PURPLES iN THE SKY...EVEN THE GOLD iN THE DANDELIONS..
...AND ALL THOSE WONDROUS COLORS iN A RAiNBOW...
...GUESS THAT'S JUST ONE OF THOSE THiNGS NOT TO BE QUESTiONED BUT ENJOYED...
Y.13
W.
P.18
B.19
W.
B.19
B.16
B.21
W
Y. 13
R.20
Y-15
R.20
G.45
LAV.12

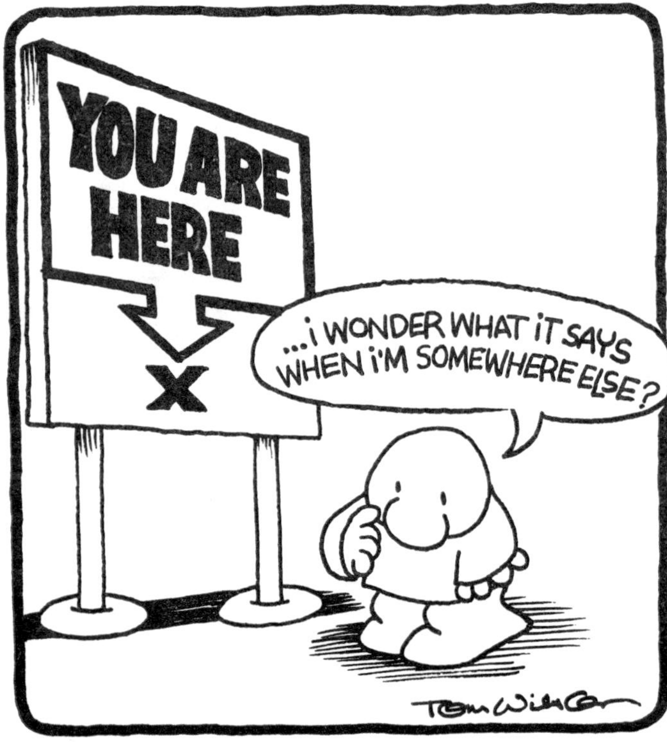
YOU ARE HERE
X
...I WONDER WHAT IT SAYS WHEN I'M SOMEWHERE ELSE?

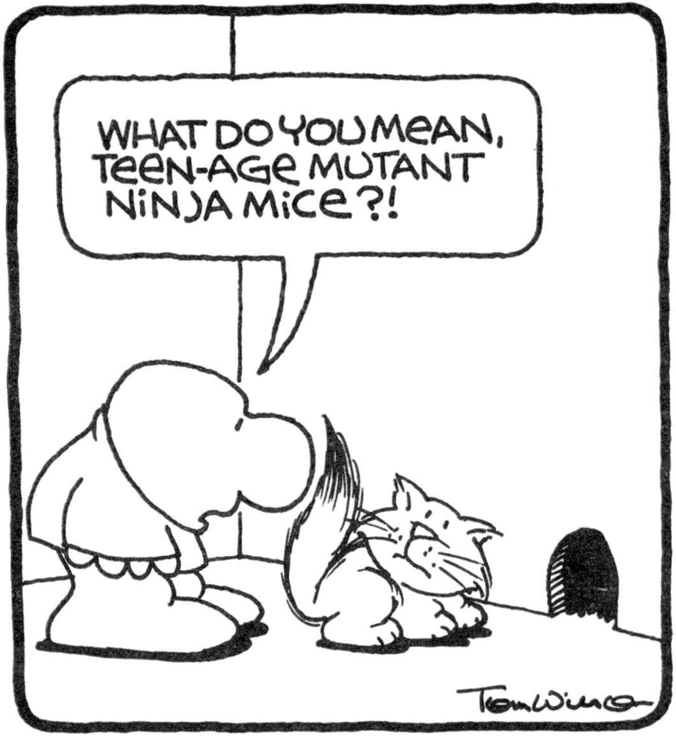
WHAT DO YOU MEAN, TEEN-AGE MUTANT NINJA MICE?!

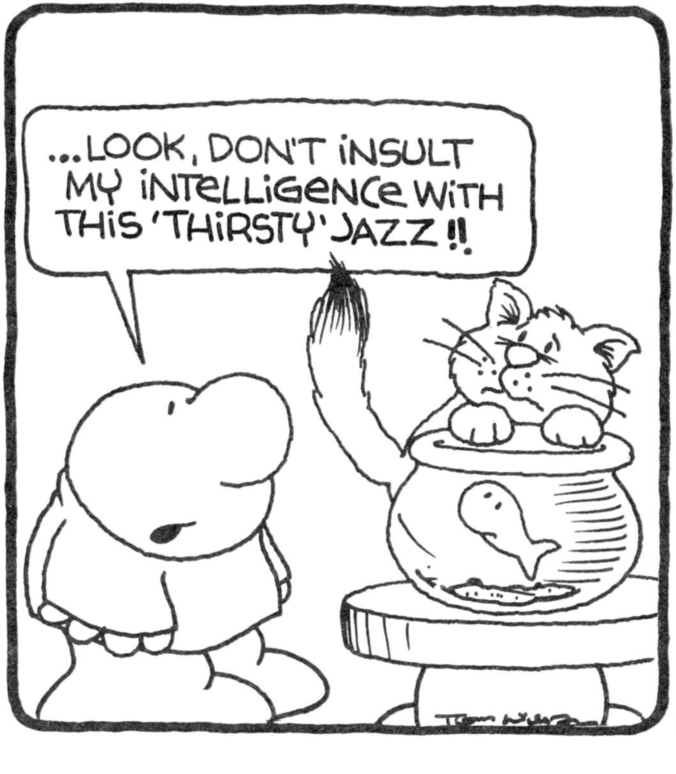
...LOOK, DON'T INSULT MY INTELLIGENCE WITH THIS 'THIRSTY' JAZZ!!

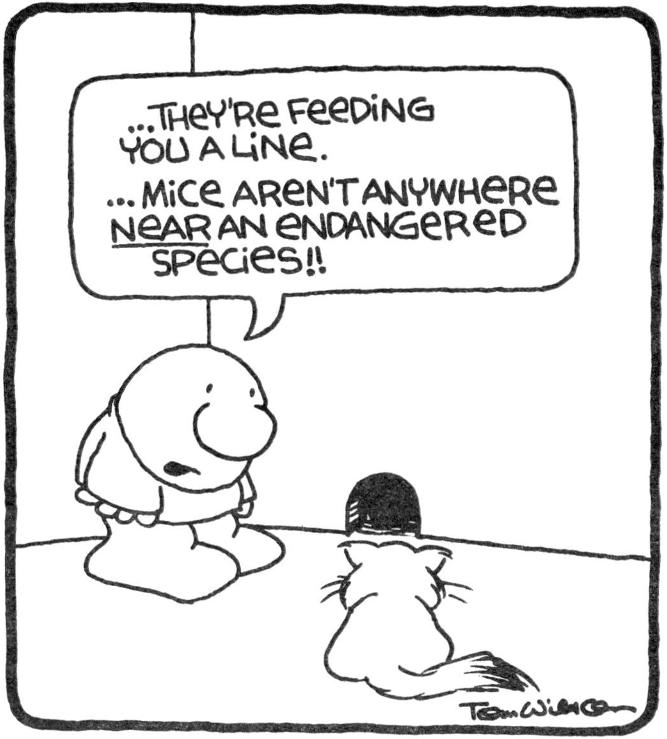
...THEY'RE FEEDING YOU A LINE.
...MICE AREN'T ANYWHERE NEAR AN ENDANGERED SPECIES!!

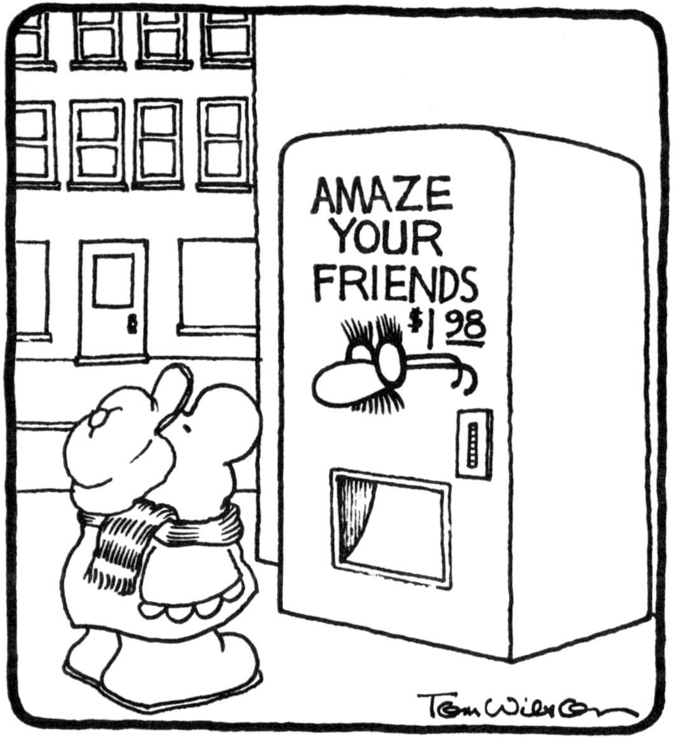
AMAZE YOUR FRIENDS
$1 98
Tom Wilson

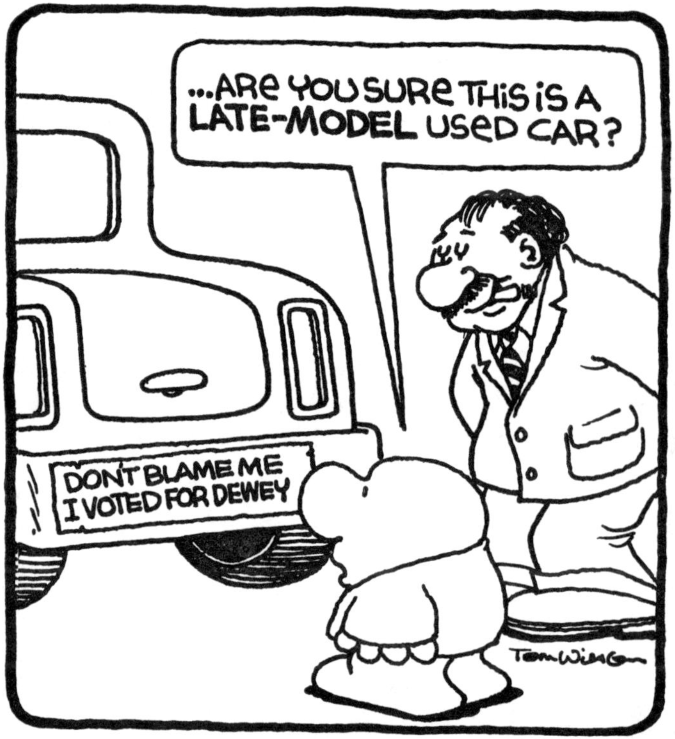
...ARE YOU SURE THIS IS A LATE-MODEL USED CAR?
DON'T BLAME ME I VOTED FOR DEWEY
Tom Wilson

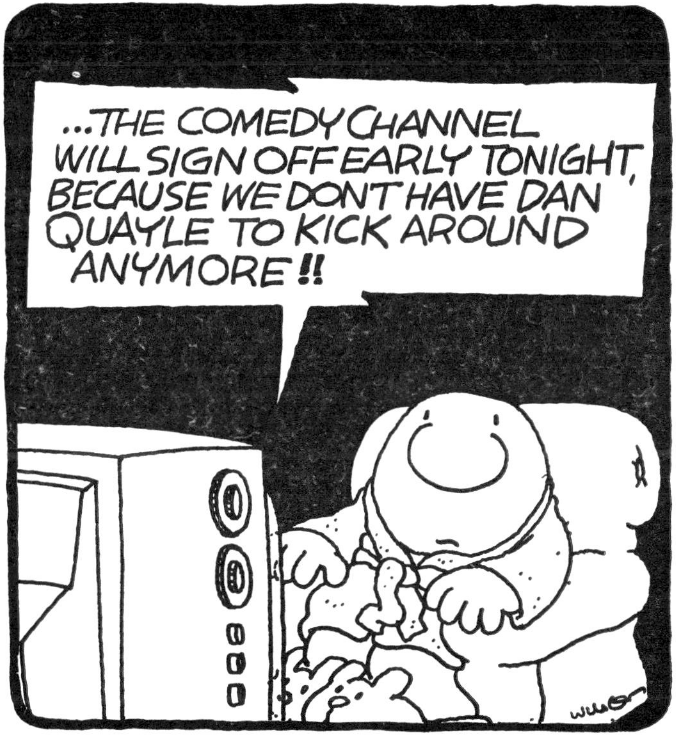
...THE COMEDY CHANNEL WILL SIGN OFF EARLY TONIGHT, BECAUSE WE DON'T HAVE DAN QUAYLE TO KICK AROUND ANYMORE!!

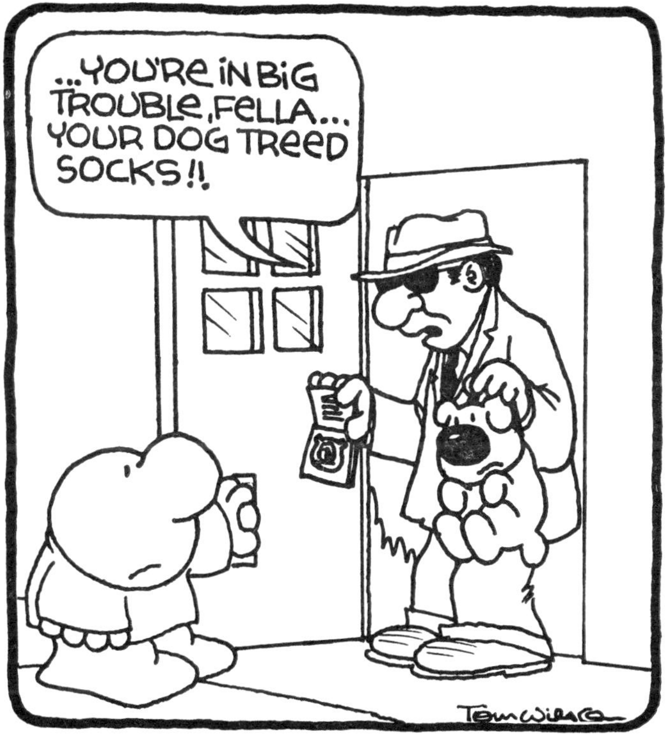
...YOU'RE IN BIG TROUBLE, FELLA... YOUR DOG TREED SOCKS!!

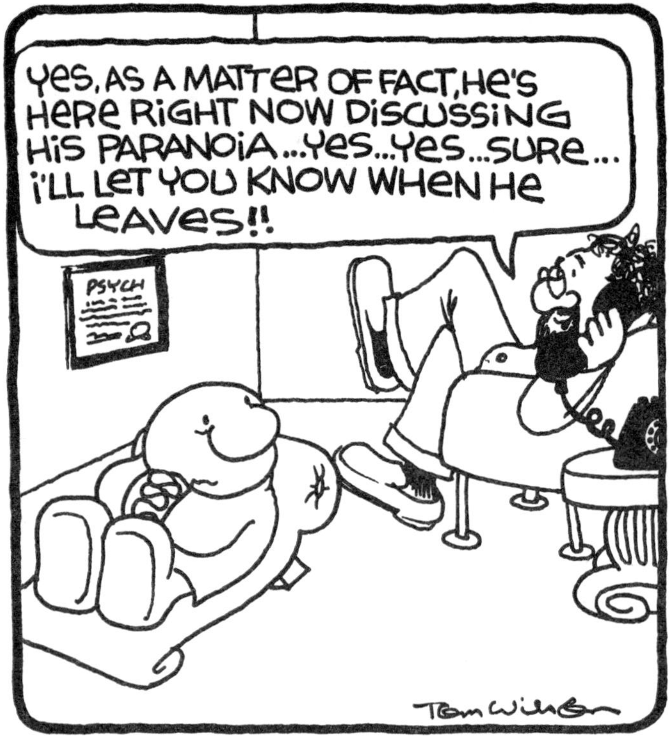
YES, AS A MATTER OF FACT, HE'S HERE RIGHT NOW DISCUSSING HIS PARANOIA...YES...YES...SURE... I'LL LET YOU KNOW WHEN HE LEAVES!!
PSYCH
Tom Wilson

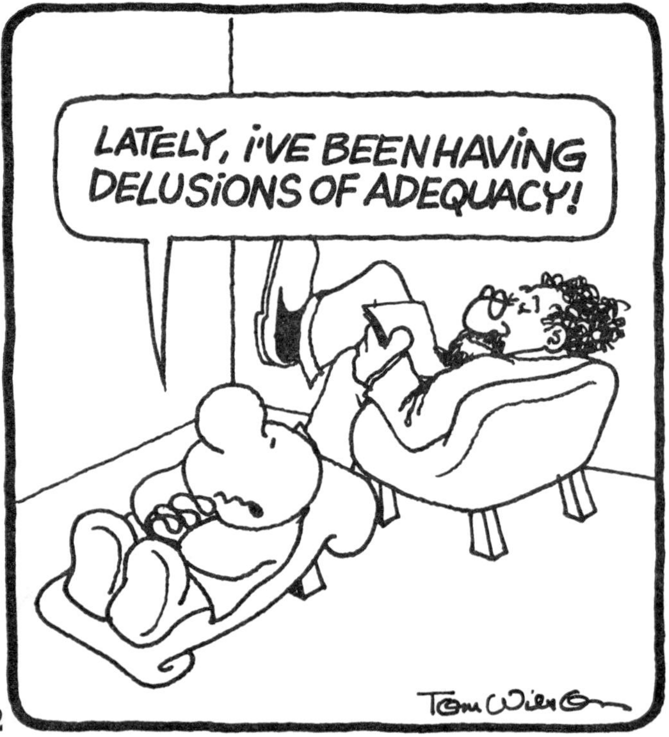
LATELY, I'VE BEEN HAVING DELUSIONS OF ADEQUACY!
Tom Wilson

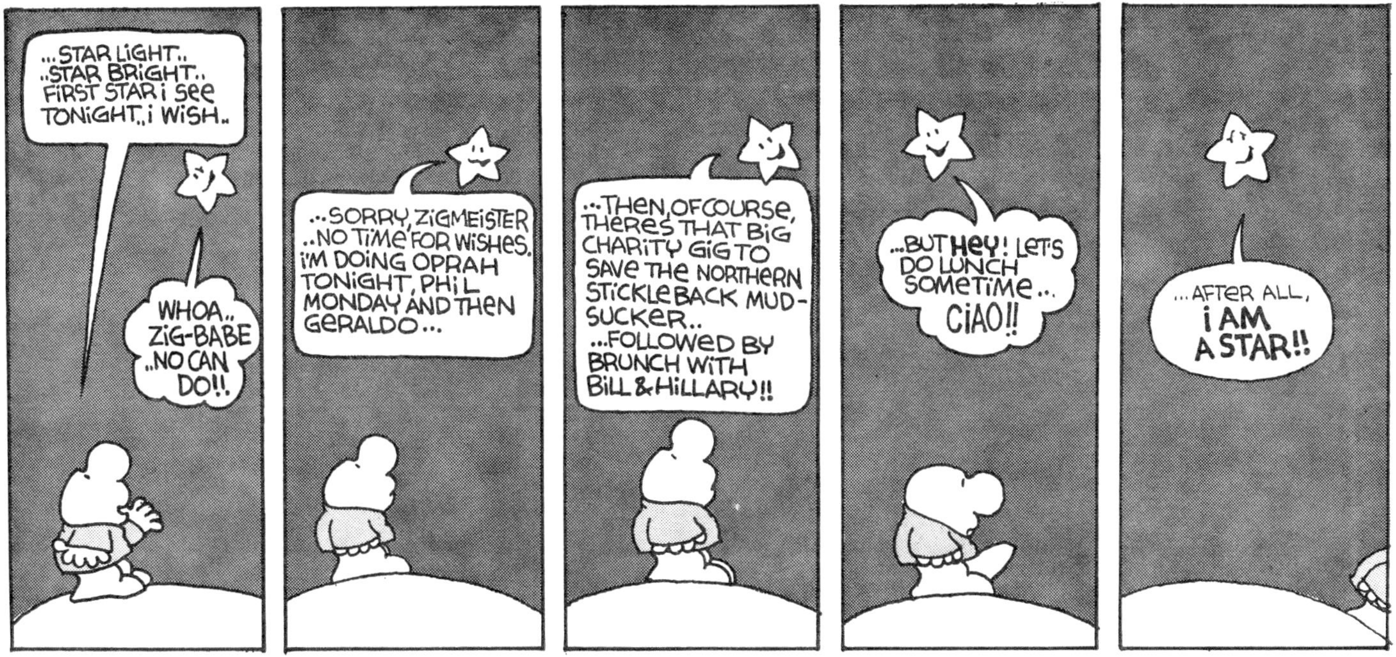
...STAR LIGHT.. ..STAR BRIGHT.. FIRST STAR I SEE TONIGHT.. I WISH..
WHOA.. ZIG-BABE ..NO CAN DO!!
...SORRY, ZIGMEISTER ..NO TIME FOR WISHES. I'M DOING OPRAH TONIGHT, PHIL MONDAY AND THEN GERALDO...
...THEN, OF COURSE, THERE'S THAT BIG CHARITY GIG TO SAVE THE NORTHERN STICKLEBACK MUD-SUCKER.. ...FOLLOWED BY BRUNCH WITH BILL & HILLARY!!
...BUT HEY! LET'S DO LUNCH SOMETIME... CIAO!!
...AFTER ALL, I AM A STAR!!

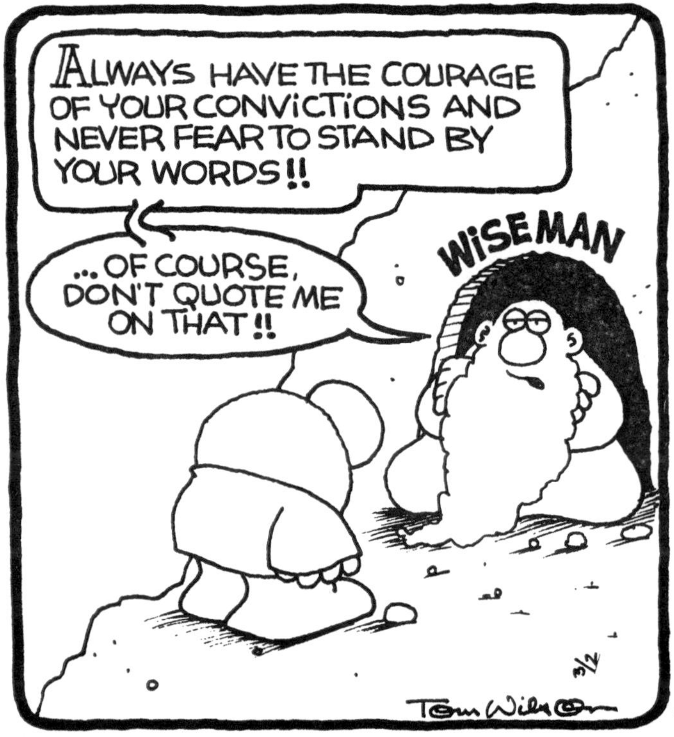
ALWAYS HAVE THE COURAGE OF YOUR CONVICTIONS AND NEVER FEAR TO STAND BY YOUR WORDS!!
...OF COURSE, DON'T QUOTE ME ON THAT!!
WISEMAN
3/2
Tom Wilson

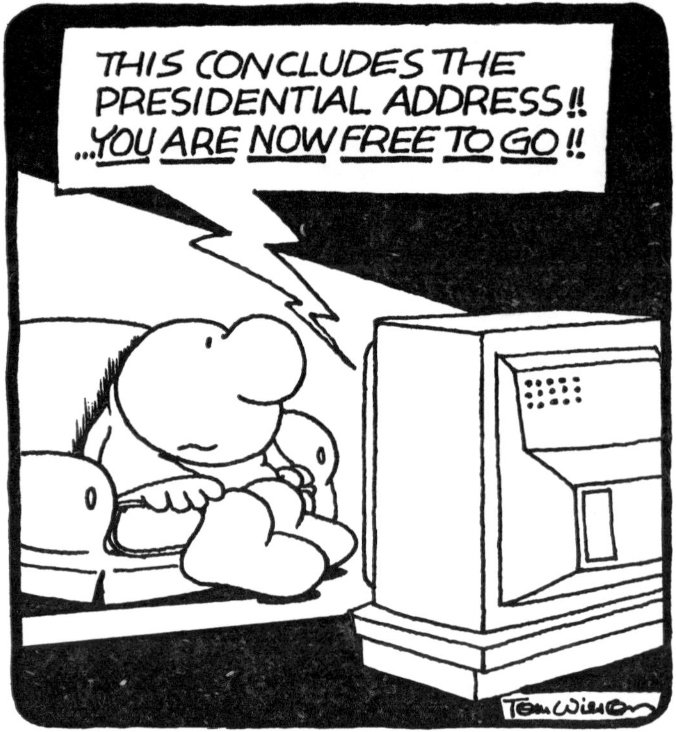
THIS CONCLUDES THE PRESIDENTIAL ADDRESS!! ...YOU ARE NOW FREE TO GO!!
Tom Wilson